I AM A
blogger.

*16 Relatable Stories of Remarkable
People Earning a Living Online*

Copyright © 2018 by Seva.

All rights reserved. No part of this book may be reproduced in any form or by any electronic or mechanical means, including information storage and retrieval systems, without permission in writing from the publisher, except by reviewers, who may quote brief passages in a review.

ISBN: 978-0-692-13084-1

Book design and layout by Charli Prangley
Written by Barrett Brooks and Kayla Hollatz
Editing by Amanda Johnson and Dani Stewart
Photography by Brandon Sullivan, Caleb Wojcik, David Sherry, Joshua Fortuna, Kambria Fischer, Mark Forbes, Maureen Cotton and Yesenia Fortuna.

Printed and bound in Surrey, England.

Published by Seva
PO Box 761
Boise, ID 83701

Visit www.seva.com

―――

This book is dedicated to our customers, our team, and all of the creators out there—past, present, and future—who inspire us to do this work every day.

— Nathan Barry, CEO of Seva

―――

Contents

Foreword by Pat Flynn	6
Introduction	10
Courtney Slazinik	14
Barron Cuadro	32
Crosby Noricks	46
Chad Collins	60
Brooke Schoenman	72
Corey Willis	86
Asad Chaudhry	100
Krista Stryker	114
Vanessa Levin	128
Dave Stuart Jr.	142
Sarah Morgan	156
Tyler James	168
Mique Provost	178
The Fantasy Footballers	192
Patty Palmer	206
Joshua Becker	220
Conclusion	234
Acknowledgments	236

FOREWORD *by Pat Flynn*

My first blog post was published when I was a sophomore in college in 2002.

It was on an ancient platform called Xanga—and, like my friends who introduced me to this "thing" called a blog, I wrote about what classes I attended that day, what I had for lunch and dinner, and how I was excited about the upcoming football game.

Nothing special.

A week later, one of my friends came up to me and said:

> *Pat . . . that chicken dish at Thai Basil—I'd never tried it before, but it was sooooooo good! Thank you!*

With a confused look, I replied:

> *Huh? Thank you for what?*

Then he explained:

> *On your blog you mentioned you had the pepper garlic chicken at Thai Basil. I tried it and it was awesome!*

That was the first time I realized how *cool* this "thing" called a blog could be.

Since then, blogging has always played an important role in my life.

When I graduated college with a degree in architecture, my effort to maintain my personal blog transformed into building a new blog related to my profession as an architect. More specifically, it became a place to keep a record of my notes for an exam that I was studying for.

Nothing special.

After passing that exam, a couple of coworkers decided to take the same exam and asked me for some help. They pitched me the idea of sitting down with them at lunch for a few months to go over the test material together.

I had a different idea.

> *Here . . . go to my blog and just start from the beginning. It'll tell you everything you need to know.*

They passed the exam a month later, and soon the entire office was using my blog to help them pass the exam, too.

That was the first time I realized how *useful* this "thing" called a blog could be.

Then 2008 happened.

The downward spiral of the US economy between 2008 and 2010 resulted in 8.8 million people losing their jobs—the most job loss since World War II.* Unfortunately, I was one of those people.

Although I had worked so hard and put in so much time and effort to further my career as an architect, I was let go.

I was angry, confused, and depressed.

I felt like I was nobody special.

I tried to get another job, but no one was hiring. I moved back home with my parents to save money and figure out what to do next. I even contemplated graduate school until the economy "worked itself out," as my parents kept promising.

*Christopher J. Goodman and Stephen M. Mance, "The 2007–09 Recession: Overview," Bureau of Labor Statistics, April 2011, https://www.bls.gov/opub/mlr/2011/04/art1full.pdf.

But I couldn't go down that path anymore.

I was on a prescribed path my entire life, doing everything the way I was supposed to—yet, I was still let go.

I wanted to do something that I had control over. Something I knew I could use to help others and potentially turn into a business one day. Something that gave me joy. So, I turned back to that "thing" I always had some fun with and was there, in the background, serving others: *my blog*.

I committed myself to becoming a blogger, and I gave my exam blog the time and attention it needed. As soon as I started to focus my efforts on taking it seriously—despite others telling me I was crazy and to "go get a real job"—something incredible happened.

People who I didn't know started to find my blog. They started to share it. They started to communicate with me and ask me questions—like I was some professor or something—which made sense because I definitely was treating them like they were my students.

I cared about them, and to my surprise, they cared back. Within a couple of months, my blog was getting five to six thousand visitors a day. Real-life people from over thirty different countries were finding my blog, and I started to receive handwritten thank-you notes in the mail.

That was the first time I realized how *impactful* and *life-changing* this "thing" called a blog could be—not just for myself, but also for those who would find my blog.

That blog turned into a six-figure business after a year, and it still serves people today at *GreenExamAcademy.com*.

I've since created several other blogs, most notably the *Smart Passive Income* blog where I share everything I learn about creating online businesses to help others make more money, save more time, and help more people.

Since becoming a blogger (and now a podcaster and video creator, too), I've realized that, as weird as it was for me to go down this particular path in life, I am not alone.

Far from it, actually.

I've met thousands of full-time and part-time creators who have found their own unique formula for combining their passion and expertise with the ability to serve and inspire others. They pair that with the words and images they share on the internet to make a meaningful living.

My story is just one of many, and hearing these kinds of stories is important because our success is limited only to what we know is possible. Similar to when the four-minute-mile barrier was broken, now we understand that, with the tools we have available to us and the stories that are there to inspire us, anybody can become their own success story.

You are about to dive into sixteen other creators' stories here in this book—and I'm not exactly sure where you're at in life right now, but I assure you that this could be the start of an amazing journey for you. For me, it took getting laid off to see what was possible. But for you, you've got this book in your hands.

I'm thankful to be at the start of so many other creators' beginnings. Maybe even yours. And I'm even more encouraged that there are communities like the one at Seva who are there to foster growth and serve others.

Here's to you and your success as a creator, and no matter what you create, make it yours and make it special.

■ *Pat Flynn*
SmartPassiveIncome.com

INTRODUCTION

You go home for the holidays, and what do your relatives want to know?

| *What are you doing for work these days?*

For many people, this is a topic they want to avoid. They don't particularly enjoy their work. Or maybe they're not particularly proud of the career they've built.

It's not that they don't want to love their work, it's just that . . . well, you've got to put dinner on the table. Not everyone can love their work, right?

But there's a group of creators out there who take their deeply loved passions to the next level—a group that's opted out of the traditional ways of doing things and opted into building a business that supports the life they want to live.

These people answer that question from their relatives with:

| *I am a blogger.*

This answer is almost always followed by an awkward silence or something like:

| *You do what? No, I asked what do you do for work. Like, how do you earn a living?*

If you earn a living online as a blogger, podcaster, or YouTuber, you may have received this kind of reaction before. And if you don't earn your living that way, well, you'll just have to trust us. It's a pretty common response.

The funny thing is, bloggers, podcasters, and vloggers are some of the most innovative entrepreneurs in the world who gain so much joy and value from their nontraditional work. They are serving people through their content, teaching what they know, and building products that change people's lives.

For some reason, when we tell stories about these people, we tend to talk a lot about money. About tactics. About conversion rates. About funnels and calls to action and sales pages.

It's almost like we believe that if we just use the tactics that successful people use, we'll be successful too. After all, that girl with the six-pack does crunches, so I better do crunches if I want a six-pack, right?

But what if the reason for her love of fitness is much deeper than great abs—what if it's the sense of joy she feels in her life, the ten hours of sleep she gets every night, the nutrition that fuels her body and mind, and the three miles she bikes to and from work every day?

When we're just getting started on a journey—whether the road to better health or building a business—we don't want to hear all of that. We want to hear that it's as simple as doing one hundred crunches every night and drinking a protein shake and—*voila!*—washboard abs. Or, to translate, we want a successful six-figure business that doesn't require us to do anything that's not fun.

The reality of what works is too human. It's too nuanced. It's too *hard*.

Let's go ahead and get this out of the way right up-front: the thing about building a business that supports the life that you want is just that—it's hard.

So, are there actually people out there earning a living online while still doing work they love?

If so, how did they get there? What's their story? What were they doing in the years before they launched their online business? And why—when they could choose to do anything—do they choose to do this work?

These were some of the questions we had when we set out to travel the country, seeking stories from a wide array of bloggers for this book. We searched for creators across as many different industries as we could find. We set the intention to tell stories of a diverse group, spanning across age, race, religion, and background. We nailed it in a few of those areas, while falling short in others.

What we found was a delightfully relatable series of stories about a remarkably inspirational group of people. They opened up and shared about their past, their dreams, their families, and so much more.

There's the high school teacher in Michigan who blogs about becoming a better classroom teacher, staying in the teaching game when it gets hard to stay positive, and—most importantly—serving all of the children in classrooms who deserve caring adults in their lives.

And then there's the photographer in Omaha who uses imagery as a way to capture the stories of her children's lives. Her blog started as a creative outlet but became a rallying point for other parents who wanted a way to cherish the fleeting moments of childhood.

There's also the men's fashion blogger who moved to New York City to be in the heart of one of the fashion capitals of the world. From the time he was a kid in Sam Goody asking his mom for a Snoop Dogg T-shirt, he realized that fashion is an outward expression of our inward identity. It's a tool for giving us self-confidence and helping us believe in ourselves.

There are sixteen of these stories in this book. All of these creators earn a full-time living from their blogs, podcasts, and YouTube channels. Whether they'll say it themselves or not, they're full-fledged entrepreneurs. In fact, most of them earn far more running their own businesses than they ever did in their previous jobs.

But this book isn't about income (even though we do share how they make money), and it isn't about tactics (even though we do share bits and pieces of business strategy). This book is about the humans behind the blogs. It's about the origin stories of the people we look up to and the emotional journey of putting yourself out there when you don't know what's going to happen next.

This book is about continuing to have an attitude of service, gratitude, and humility even in the face of success beyond what you ever could have imagined. What you'll find is that the success these bloggers have experienced is largely about the years they spent before they ever started a blog or business, the years spent becoming better people, exploring what mattered to them, and eventually landing on a topic they cared so much about that they just had to share it with others.

This is the story of earning a living as a blogger, and there's much more to it than you might expect. The commonality between these bloggers is not the tactics they use or the ways they make money—it's the meaning they find in the work they do and how that shows through the way they serve others.

> *So, yes, Grandma . . . I am a blogger. That's how I earn a living. But more importantly, that's how I make a difference.*

We hope you enjoy reading these sixteen stories as much as we've enjoyed telling them. But more than anything, we hope when you close the back cover of this book you walk away with one very clear message: you are every bit as capable, worthy, and ready to take the leap as the people in this book.

Will you?

Barrett Brooks
COO of Seva

Courtney Slazinik

Teacher. Photographer. Wife. Mom. Blogger.

WORDS BY BARRETT BROOKS • PHOTOGRAPHY BY CALEB WOJCIK

With her best friend's fourth child on the way, Courtney Slazinik asked if she could photograph the delivery.

She wanted to be there in that moment when a mother sees her child and when a father holds his baby in his arms for the first time—to capture the tears, the challenge, the beauty, and the joy of the miracle of birth.

A few months later, Courtney got the call to be at the hospital, and soon she was in the middle of the action: "Breathe!" . . . "Push!" . . . "Keep breathing!"

As the hours passed, Courtney captured each moment. She caught the face of the excited dad and the face of her friend as she labored to bring her child into the world. And then she finally captured one of her favorite photos she's ever taken to this day: the moment a mother is handed her child for the first time.

It was in that intimate moment, just after the umbilical cord was cut, that Courtney realized just how much power that camera in her hand could carry.

> *It was the first moment that she saw him, and she's holding him up and she's crying, and it was just such a magical thing. And every time I look at that picture I get super teary-eyed. I think, "Oh my gosh I was there for that and this was a gift I have to give to you."*

That photo, and the thousands of other photos she's taken over the years, are why Courtney started her business, Click It Up a Notch®. It's the chance to give the gift of memories to other parents just like her.

Her commitment to helping parents capture those special moments as their children grow up is what's turned her "little side project" into a six-figure business that was named one of the top five blogs for "momtographers" on the web by *The Huffington Post*.

If you were to look at the metrics driving Courtney's business in 2017, you'd never guess that she never really thought about becoming an entrepreneur.

In fact, she's still hesitant to acknowledge that she's not just an entrepreneur, but also a successful one at that.

The Teacher

> *Growing up, I wanted to be an elementary school teacher. That was always my dream—to have children and be an elementary school teacher.*

And that's what she did. Coming out of college, Courtney became a third- and fifth-grade classroom teacher. And while she loved so much about her job, the most magical moments were when she saw a student's eyes light up after learning something new.

One such moment in particular came after testing was done for the year; her fifth-graders were working on a book project.

With the pressure of state testing behind them, Courtney got creative by asking her students to act as if they were Oprah (who, at this time, was still on TV every afternoon) by interviewing one of the characters from the book. Each of the kids performed their own interview. Afterwards, one student turned to Courtney and said, "This is the best thing we've done all year. I loved working on this."

That was the magic of teaching: the transformation of learning something mundane into capturing imaginations.

Unfortunately, classroom teaching—the actual impact on the students—is such a small part of what a teacher deals with.

It wears on you.

2003 Becomes a teacher

And after a long, hard year teaching in Mississippi, it had definitely worn down Courtney. The stress was growing, and she was losing touch with what drew her to teaching to begin with.

So when her husband, Ian, got wind that his job in the Air Force was taking them on a new adventure in a new city, they decided Courtney should take a break before heading back to the classroom.

And then they got pregnant with their first daughter, Kate.

The Mom

The only thing that Courtney had wanted to be, other than a teacher, was a mom. Her mom was a stay-at-home mom and Courtney wanted to offer the same to her children.

So when they found out they were pregnant, Courtney knew there would be no going back to the classroom—at least, not for now.

She focused on becoming a great mom, just like her mom had been. Along the way she picked up her first camera, a point-and-shoot, and started using it to document the experience of raising her first child. The photos weren't great, but they were capturing memories.

Kate was an easy baby. Courtney loved taking care of her little human so much so that shortly after Kate's first birthday, they became pregnant with their second child.

Little did she know that Emma's birth would also set her on the path to starting a business.

The Photographer

After an unexpected camera mishap with her husband and an ill-placed chair in the delivery room during her second daughter's birth, Courtney upgraded from a point-and-shoot camera to a DSLR, the first step in professional photography gear.

With her new DSLR, Courtney went on to take almost 4,000 photos in Emma's first three months of life. She saw a huge difference between these photos and the ones she had taken on her old point-and-shoot. But as she looked at one of her friend's photos, she saw an even bigger difference.

Assuming a DSLR was all it took to take great photos, she asked her friend how she made them better. Her friend encouraged her to get a quality lens to start shooting on manual mode.

And just like that, Courtney was introduced to a whole new world of knowledge and information. She knew almost immediately that she had found the passion she wanted to dive deep on.

2009 Daughter Emma is born

2010 Starts Project 365

Courtney Slazinik

Her friend started coming over every couple of weeks and helped Courtney learn how to take photos on manual mode. She immediately started learning about the fundamentals of her camera: aperture, shutter speed, and ISO.

With her new knowledge, Courtney started something called Project 365 with a group of fellow moms online. Their goal was for each person to take at least one photo every day for a year.

To share her photos and her learnings, Courtney started a family blog to post her photos. And as her photos got better, her friends started reaching out asking how she did it.

Courtney brushed it off as her friends being kind. But then she got one email in particular that said, "I'll pay you to teach me how to do this."

> " I'm going to start a new blog, and I'm going to make money from it.

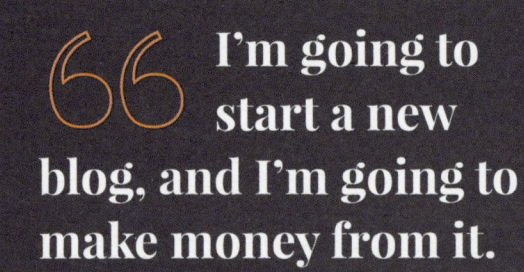

Then she started putting two and two together.

> I started thinking, "Oh there's an interest? I love teaching, and I love photography . . . I could put these two together and get to help people, still learn about photography myself, and still get to teach people." It was kind of the best of both worlds.

By that time, Courtney had been a stay-at-home mom for almost three years. She had started to lose her sense of identity and was struggling with the lack of affirmation and praise that comes from raising two children under the age of three. It's a thankless job—and, as Courtney puts it,

> Nobody says, "You rocked changing that diaper today."

She loved her kids and she loved being a mom, but she needed more. She needed a creative outlet—something to give her a sense of affirmation and purpose.

Standing in her kitchen, Courtney remembers calling her best friend one day and sharing an idea.

> I'm going to start a new blog, and I'm going to make money from it.

They both laughed. But it wasn't a joke. Courtney was serious.

The Entrepreneur

On the advice from her parents, Courtney named her blog *Click it Up a Notch*®. She had a name. Now it was time to set a goal.

> I remember saying to my husband, "Wouldn't that be crazy if I made $200 a month?"

So that was her goal in the beginning: start a blog and earn $200 a month.

She started with a paper editorial calendar, writing down her ideas for blog posts that could help other moms like her take great photos of their kids. It was 2010, one year after her second daughter was born, and nap time became sacred.

> *I told my friends, "Don't call me during nap time. Don't try and make plans with me during nap time."*

She only had an hour or two to work on *Click It Up a Notch*®, and she didn't want any distractions. But an hour wasn't enough each day, so for the first year, Courtney stayed up late at night to work on the blog.

She would take the next post from her editorial calendar and type it up, making a list of the photos she needed to take of the kids the next day to illustrate the teaching in the post.

A few months in, wondering how long this was going to last while still being supportive, Ian said in passing, "Oh, you know, it'll be nice when you go back to work when the kids are in school."

Courtney, like any determined entrepreneur, replied, "What? I'm not going back to work. I do this now. If I can figure out a way to make this make money, I'd like to keep staying at home."

It was important to Courtney to find a way to earn a living doing work she loved while also being a huge part of her kids' lives. She read online that any blog takes at least three years to get to the point where it could create an income.

"I want to try this for three years. I'm committing to myself that I will not quit for that long," she told Ian. She was determined to give this thing a real shot, and Ian supported her 100%.

Until she got pregnant with their third daughter and the morning sickness hit.

I'm Quitting

Due to the terrible exhaustion and morning sickness that came with her third pregnancy, Courtney had reached what she thought was her limit, but the universe, or God, wasn't done with her yet.

> **"** I want to try this for three years. I'm committing to myself that I will not quit for that long.

TAMRON®, a Japanese maker of camera lenses, was recommended to check out *Click it Up a Notch®* by one of Courtney's photographer friends. It was just shortly after Courtney declared she was quitting when she got an email from them asking her to partner with them to help promote a new lens.

"Okay, I'm not quitting," Courtney immediately told herself.

Creating Her First Product

With the new momentum from the TAMRON® partnership, Courtney started working on her first product—an eBook, *The Unexpected Everyday*—that combined some of her top learnings into a cohesive guide to getting started as a momtographer.

> Courtney estimates that she took between 60,000 and 70,000 photographs from when she started the business to when she sold her first eBook.

When it was finished in 2013, Courtney knew she needed to promote it to her audience but had no idea how to "launch a product." So she did what any normal person would do: she sent an email to her blog followers and said, "Hey, I made this eBook for you. Wanna buy it?"

Yes, they did. In the forty-eight hours after sending that first email, Courtney sold $3,000 in revenue from one eBook. That success is directly related to the genuine connection she made with her audience.

Courtney had spent nearly three years writing blog posts for free, sharing from a place of genuine interest and care for documenting her children's lives. She had a deep desire to become a better photographer and share what she learned with others to help them do the same.

2013 Launches first eBook

Courtney estimates that she took between 60,000 and 70,000 photographs from when she started the business to when she sold her first eBook.

This authentic approach resonated with other moms, so it was only natural that a subset of them would trust Courtney enough to know that her first product would have their best interest in mind. At that point, spending $22 on a product created by a person you know, like, and trust is not a big leap.

This marked another major turning point in Courtney's story. She knew she needed to figure out how to do product launches as best she could to truly grow her business.

Reflecting on this time in the business, Courtney realizes this was when she first understood that this was about more than just a blog, more than just a creative outlet. She had created a job out of thin air, and it was becoming an engine for paying for vacations, Christmas presents, and savings for her family.

> *It's a pretty crazy feeling to think, "Yeah, I just invented this." I made it up in my head, and now I have a business.*

As Courtney continued to build her audience through blogging and sharing tutorials, she saw new opportunities to grow the business with live online workshops.

These workshops would be a chance to take what she was teaching on the blog and in her eBooks and deliver it to a live group in an engaging way. She'd be able to interact directly with her audience and help them grow.

As she was getting ready for the launch of her first workshop, Courtney got the kids off to school like normal, reminding them to ride the bus home that day so that she could finish preparing for the sale to go live.

> # What am I doing?
>
> # Why am I even doing this?

That afternoon she picked up her phone to hear the principal of the school on the other end of the line saying, "I have your daughter here at school. It seems you may have forgotten to pick her up."

Mortified, Courtney rushed to pick up her daughter.

Sitting in bed that evening, Courtney started crying.

> *What am I doing?*
> *Why am I even doing this?*

That moment of questioning and reflection was one of many for Courtney. She had to take a step back and make sure she didn't let her entrepreneurial side completely take over. The whole point of *Click It Up a Notch*® was to be a great mom and to do work she cared deeply about. It was a good reminder.

The workshop launch went off as planned. Courtney sold fifty spots in less than twenty-four hours, earning $30,000! It was a huge success and would become a blueprint for launching new workshops and relaunching existing workshops over time.

> *I just remember my husband coming home from work and us both jumping up and down. It took a long time to get there, and I had sacrificed a lot. Obviously, you know, I left a kid at school one day, but it was a huge moment.*

It was her proudest moment in the business, and she had created a model that would work for her going forward. Her eBooks and courses would become the core of what has allowed her to build a six-figure business. But the most valuable lesson of all was that Courtney knew she wanted a better sense of balance in her life going forward.

> **This business has changed how I see myself, how I see raising daughters in this world.**

A Day in the Life

Now, a typical week for Courtney looks like a repeating cycle of splitting her days between building her business and being a great mom. She never wants her daughters to look back and remember her glued to her computer.

To help with this, she's set a rule for herself that she never starts work before getting the girls off to school.

Her day begins with packing lunches, making breakfast, and taking her kids to the bus. She then works from home through the day until they come back when

Courtney shifts her focus 100% to being an engaged mom. She shuttles the kids to their activities, makes dinner, and then they play, read, and enjoy time together before bed.

She tries hard not to work at night anymore—connecting with her husband is more important.

She still has her hard days when she needs help. When those days come, she asks for friends or family to help watch the girls on occasion, and her husband is there as always to support and work side by side with Courtney.

The Role Model

Courtney sees the secret sauce of *Click It Up a Notch®* very clearly: it's how she relates to the people in her audience—because she has been in their shoes.

When Courtney got her first camera, she had no idea how to take good photographs, but she knew she wanted to capture those little moments with her kids.

It wasn't always easy.

Courtney was lucky to have a friend who taught her how to get started, but most people don't have that. In some ways, Courtney has become that friend for each person in her audience. She's that friend one step ahead on the same journey, sharing what she's learning as she goes, and that has made all the difference.

The business success has been great. She's proud of it, and she has no plans of stopping any time soon. But when asked about what matters the most from her story and the story of *Click It Up a Notch®*, she summons a memory from the not-so-distant past:

> *I remember I was signing up for my first big class. As I was typing in my information, one of my daughters comes in and asks what I'm doing. I tell her, "I'm investing in my education because I own a business and someday you can own a business. You can do that."*

She tells me, "Mmm, I want to be a zookeeper."

I tell her, "You can do that too! That's cool!"

This business has changed how I see myself, how I see raising daughters in this world.

To Courtney, being able to serve as a role model to her girls is more valuable than anything else. She shows them they can be strong *and* caring. They can work *and* be a mom. They can start something from scratch, or they can be a zookeeper. But whatever they do, they'll never have to question whether their mom chased her own dream.

■

The Business Today

Revenue Breakdown

80% Courses   **10%** Affiliate sales   **10%** eBooks

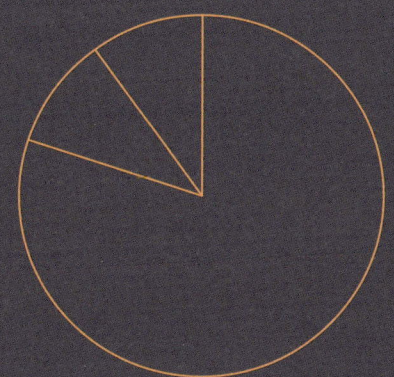

Launch Success

2013 — **$3,000** Sales from the launch of first eBook in 48 hours

2015 — **$30,000** Sales from the launch of first workshop in 24 hours

By the Numbers

$179,000
Income generated in 2017

132,000
Unique website visitors per month

62,000
Email subscribers

Products & Services

- Beginners Guide to Manual Mode course
- Beginners Guide to Lightroom course
- *The Unexpected Everyday* eBook
- *The Styled Photographer* eBook
- The Clean Collection presets

clickitupanotch.com

Barron Cuadro

Writer. Style Entrepreneur. Blogger.

WORDS BY KAYLA HOLLATZ • PHOTOGRAPHY BY CALEB WOJCIK

In fourth grade, Barron Cuadro walked into Sam Goody, a music store at the mall, with his mom beside him. Flipping through the racks of clothes, he found an extra large Snoop Dogg T-shirt.

Taking the shirt off the hanger, he held it up to his body and grinned at his mom. He didn't care that it was a few sizes too big, passing just below his knees and hanging well over his shoulders. He was too busy strategizing a way to convince his mom to buy the shirt.

Barron's mom, however, didn't share his look of excitement. She shook her head with a hearty laugh and said, "You are not buying that." To his disappointment, he knew he would have to leave the store without the Snoop Dogg shirt.

> *The shirt made me feel something. Style is an emotional response to a piece of clothing that you see. As I grew up, I was always really experimental with my style and the stuff I wore.*

Decades later, Barron admits that while he wouldn't choose this shirt from the clothing rack today, it gave him a similar feeling that he now gets when looking at a well-made tie or pocket square.

For Barron, fashion has always given him an outlet for creative expression. Personal style came naturally to him, but he quickly realized that other young professional men had difficulty dressing themselves in a way that felt authentic and presentable.

This led him to start a blog that would later become the catalyst of his business, but before that could happen, he had to recognize the need for his unique skills by immersing himself in the corporate world.

Barron's Earliest Career Path

During college, Barron landed an internship at CNET, a tech product review company based in San Francisco. He worked as a website developer for two additional years after finishing his internship and graduating from college.

Like many corporate positions, Barron felt like he was living Groundhog Day over and over again when he woke up every morning. After a fifteen minute walk to work, he would start working on web development projects until boredom kicked in. Then he'd walk to the coffee machine for a change of scenery and go back to his desk to answer emails.

Barron remembers watching the clock every afternoon, waiting for 5:00 p.m. to finally roll around so he could go home to unwind. The monotonous rhythm only got worse a year into his job, so he decided to start exploring other career paths in 2008.

He played around with the idea of getting a job at an agency, starting one of his own, or freelancing as a side hustle, but nothing felt like the perfect fit.

2008 Starts exploring other career paths

He knew he wanted to be a business owner but was unsure of the type of business he wanted to run. As a kid, he and his friends dreamed about opening a brick-and-mortar store or pursuing real estate, but the rise of internet-based businesses in 2009 piqued his interest.

Inspired by Fizzle and Gary Vaynerchuk, Barron felt that starting a blog would be his best step forward. He didn't intend for his blog to become a business right away, but he regularly imagined what it could grow into down the road.

> " Style is an emotional response to a piece of clothing that you see.

Although Barron knew a lot about website development, he was more interested in creating a side project that highlighted another skill. He thought back to how many people had asked him over the years for style advice, and a new idea was born.

> *I grew up with friends and colleagues who would ask me style-related questions, and I never really thought twice about it. But then I realized if these guys have really basic questions about what to wear, there have to be other guys out there who have similar questions.*

Already knowing how to develop a website, Barron began writing content for his new blog, *Effortless Gent*, that would help other men look and feel their best through personal style tips.

He also talked with his now-wife Kate about the blog idea, and she loved it. In fact, the first thing she noticed about Barron was his personal style. As a fashion designer herself, Kate liked the way Barron was dressed when he approached her during their daily commute on the city train. A year into the relationship, she told him that his seemingly simple outfit helped him make a great first impression.

> **I didn't know what *Effortless Gent* was going to be or if it would even be successful, but I wasn't too worried about that. I just wanted to make sure I got something out there.**

Hoping to help other men feel that same confidence, Barron set out to create a platform to make style more accessible for the everyday professional.

Launch of *Effortless Gent*

Knowing that image and perception is important in men's style, Barron followed the same approach when building his new online platform. To make sure his site reached the level of design and function he wanted, it took Barron two months to fully build.

He created the website on the side of his full-time job at CNET, which proved to be difficult as he started to ramp-up his blog content publishing. After working all day, he would come home to eat dinner with Kate and then work on *Effortless Gent* from 7:00 p.m. to 2:00 a.m.

While Barron knew he didn't want to work late night hours forever, he knew the sacrifice in his first year would help him build a solid foundation.

> *I didn't know what* Effortless Gent *was going to be or if it would even be successful, but I wasn't too worried about that. I just wanted to make sure I got something out there. I figured I would take it one step at a time and see where it would lead.*

Sustaining this slow and steady pace, Barron continued to work on the website as he improved the design and attracted more readers. In his first year of blogging, Instagram and Facebook weren't big traffic drivers, but Twitter helped him build relationships early on.

Instead of focusing on social media marketing, he focused heavily on creating valuable content for his email list. Barron noticed that staying in constant communication with his email subscribers helped him provide better content because many of his ideas were coming directly from what his audience said they needed.

In his second year of blogging, Barron decided to create a small eBook on how to dress stylishly. Before writing a word, he surveyed his email subscribers to see what questions they had about style. These questions helped him create a simple outline for the eBook so he could start writing with confidence.

While writing his eBook, Barron decided to publish a blog post every week to talk about what he was creating and how the process was going. After finishing it and making it ready for purchase at twenty-five dollars, Barron was shocked at how well it sold.

The eBook generated enough money during its launch to encourage Barron to think about quitting his full-time job to pursue *Effortless Gent* and freelancing full-time.

Quitting His Nine-to-Five Job

Barron didn't go into the process of creating his first digital product with the goal of quitting his day job, but that's exactly what happened. With the extra income generated from the blog and eBook sales, Barron was faced with a big decision in his second year of blogging. Was it time to take the leap?

Quitting his job felt less risky because he knew how marketable his skills were as a web developer and designer. After handing in his two weeks' notice, his boss told him that CNET would have a position open for him if he ever decided to come back.

> *I didn't feel like I had too much to lose. I just knew I wanted to go forward and build* Effortless Gent. *I didn't really have a specific plan, but I knew that if I could sell this eBook and make $4000 to $5000 in a few weeks, I could continue to market it and create more products that would sell eventually.*

Knowing that he had options, Barron took a step toward *Effortless Gent* and picked up a few short-term freelance gigs to generate a more stable income while he focused more attention on his website.

Surprisingly Lucrative Income Streams

When Barron started his blog, he never considered pursuing brand sponsorships or affiliate partnerships as a part of his business model. He was always more focused on creating valuable free content on his blog and providing digital products as an upsell.

> "I didn't feel like I had too much to lose. I just knew I wanted to go forward and build *Effortless Gent*."

> **You can have a profitable online business if you are able to buckle down and know what your strengths are.**

After launching his first eBook, Barron wrote a few more eBooks priced anywhere between ten to fifteen dollars while also creating an online men's style course at a higher price point around ninety-nine dollars. Digital products seemed to be a good moneymaker until he began experimenting with other income streams.

Instead of only focusing on digital products, Barron thought about creating a physical product with a fashion line for *Effortless Gent*. Since Kate is a fashion designer, they both collaborated to create a men's line called *Fifth & Brannan* in 2014.

They worked with various factories and suppliers to make the dream a reality. After testing different styles in the market during their initial launch, Barron found that accessories like ties and pocket squares were the most successful. It's been one of the most rewarding projects Barron has worked on.

2014 Creates men's fashion line *Fifth & Brannan*

> *I wouldn't have done the fashion line if I didn't have my wife. Selling physical goods is very different from digital products. You have to actually carry inventory, worry about patterns and fabrics, and so many other little details I never would've thought about. It was definitely helpful having her as a partner since she has plenty of experience in the fashion design world.*

The fashion line was getting off the ground around the same time that Barron and Kate decided to move from San Francisco to New York. As they settled into their new life in New York, they decided to press pause on the fashion line until they could focus more of their attention on it.

Even with taking a step back from *Fifth & Brannan*, Barron's blog continued to flourish as more collaboration requests came pouring in. After becoming an influencer in men's fashion, Barron was perfectly positioned for brand sponsorships. Barron only got serious about brand sponsorships and affiliate partnerships about four years into his business.

As he began working with well-known brands, he created strict guidelines so he was only working with advertisers that were a natural fit with his audience and values.

2015 — Shifts focus to brand collaborations

The biggest income generator for *Effortless Gent* is now brand sponsorships, making up 80% of his total income. While it may have surprised Barron how lucrative these collaborations could be, he's now incorporated more sponsored content into his strategy while working with advertisers that he already loves.

The other 20% of Barron's income comes from digital products like courses and eBooks. Ideally, he would like to create an equal split between the two main income streams while focusing more attention on digital products, which is his main business goal for the next few years.

Barron's Life and Business Today

Barron is thankful to have those long nights of working until 2:00 a.m. behind him. Now he can take advantage of a more balanced lifestyle.

If he had to describe his lifestyle in one word, he would choose relaxed. He usually starts his days at 7:30 a.m. and goes to the gym before coming home to work. He starts with answering a few emails and talking to his blog editor about what he's working on that week. He'll also talk to his agent to see what brand sponsorship collaborations he has coming up.

Much of his time is focused on creating great content for his loyal blog readers. As a writer, he loves staying in his zone of genius. He's also more focused on design and branding than ever, attributing his visual style as one of the main reasons why he's been able to differentiate himself.

Rather than sharing his outfit of the day, Barron has carved out a unique niche for himself by catering to men who want a more personal approach to style. Instead of trying to appeal to the masses, he provides valuable content for the readers he already has. This has helped him attract more readers over time.

> *You can have a profitable online business if you are able to buckle down and know what your strengths are. Just play to those things.*

Like many entrepreneurs, Barron still struggles with chasing new ideas, but he's still focused on doing what he does best. In the next few years, he wants to focus more energy on video marketing and becoming more comfortable on camera. He's also excited about creating one-on-one and group coaching opportunities so he can test the waters with service-based offerings.

Barron has even bigger dreams for where he wants to take *Effortless Gent* now that he's settled into New York. With his supportive wife by his side, he feels as though he can accomplish anything—and do it in style.

The Business Today

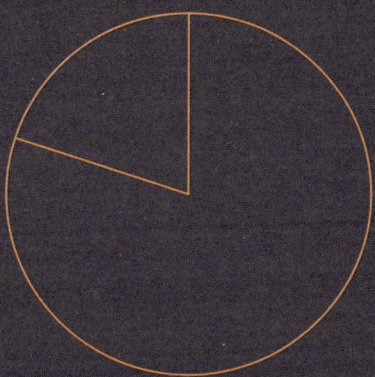

Revenue Breakdown

80%
Brand collaborations & ad/affiliate income

20%
Digital products

Launch Success

= 100 books

$13,000
Earned from the sale of 500 eBooks in three months

By the Numbers

1,500,000
Unique website visitors in 2017

17,720
Email subscribers

2,300,000
Pageviews in 2017

$7,500
Average monthly revenue for 2017

Products & Services

- *Match Clothes Like A Pro* eBook
- Personal styling sessions
- Smart Sharp Style course
- Brand sponsorships

effortlessgent.com

Crosby Noricks

Fashion PR Professional. Educator. Entrepreneur. Blogger.

WORDS BY KAYLA HOLLATZ • PHOTOGRAPHY BY KAMBRIA FISCHER

T he chime of the doorbell signaled that a new creative exploration was about to happen.

When five-year-old Crosby opened the door, her grandmother poked out her head from behind a large cardboard box stuffed with unfolded clothes spewing from the top—all found at yet another estate sale. Her grandmother had a reputation for scoring the best finds, much to Crosby's enjoyment.

Once her grandmother set the box down, Crosby began to take out every garment and accessory piece by piece. Every estate sale box was like a treasure chest, and Crosby didn't waste any time exploring its contents.

She carefully picked up a piece of costume jewelry out of a vintage keepsake box and clasped it around her neck. The ruby-colored jewels reflected the light in the room on the walls.

Crosby, looking at her mother dressed in an old fur coat and loud colored tights, smiled sweetly as she put on rhinestone-studded sunglasses and walked along the perimeter of the closet as if she was an Old Hollywood movie star.

But the estate-sale finds weren't only for Crosby and her mother to enjoy.

Proudly calling her childhood home the "dress-up box," Crosby would invite her neighbors and elementary school friends to come over and play dress-up while doing makeovers until wee hours in the night.

> *From a very early age, clothing was about fantasy, exploration, play, and becoming a different person. As I grew up, it also became a way to differentiate and . . . be a little bit artistic.*

Crosby's favorite childhood pastime inspired an even bigger passion: self-expression through fashion.

She fondly remembers running in and out of nearby flea markets and thrift shops with her mother. At just eight years old, one seemingly ordinary trip to the mall with her mother would inspire Crosby's first business idea: to open a store called Basics that sold basic-shaped clothing in every color.

> *I think Basics was my first clear business idea. "Here's the opportunity in the marketplace. This is the solution. This is my problem, and here's a way that we could create a solution."*

Her boutique idea would later bring life to dozens of other business ideas as Crosby started to explore opportunities outside of the status quo, largely inspired by her mother's nontraditional mind-set.

Always dressing slightly unconventional and encouraging her children to travel the world, Crosby's mother was a risk-taker in her own right. No experience or dream was out of reach for her mother—and she passed down this sentiment to Crosby at a very young age.

Before she decided on a major in college, Crosby was inspired by her mother to simply take classes that interested her and find a direction from there. Her mother's free spirit and spontaneous creativity gave Crosby the courage to build a life for herself outside the box.

Crosby didn't know it then, but this mind-set would lead her to become the driven self-starter, entrepreneur, and editorial director she is today.

The Eternal Student

Immediately following her high school graduation, Crosby found herself involved in media studies at Pitzer College.

Much to her dismay, the media studies program had no fashion, marketing, or public relations focus, but Crosby was determined to find a way to fit her passion

1987 First business idea, Basics

into her degree. She petitioned to study at the London College of Fashion for a semester, but quickly found that the American program was separate from the well-known London fashion program.

When Crosby graduated, she contemplated working in the wardrobe department for film and television crews, but was soon deflated to see how many entry-level stylists were asked to work for free on spec. With financial independence as one of her core values, she wanted to find a way to advance her career while making substantial payments toward her student loans.

This was around the time Crosby started her first website, named messycloset.net. Its mission was to create a dedicated online space for professional women in creative industries who wanted to share who they were and connect with one another.

> *I thought, "I can build a space and resources that would help individuals succeed professionally." At the time, I didn't connect it but now I see where I was going with it all—there's a branding and presentation component to standing out and getting noticed.*

After applying and being accepted to two different graduate programs and a move to Barcelona, Crosby eventually landed in San Diego State's top-ranked communications graduate program in 2004.

Tasked with creating her master's thesis toward the end of her graduate education, she was encouraged by her advisor to study the fast-paced, somewhat hidden, and always misunderstood world of fashion PR.

> *The minute you add "fashion" to something, it's suddenly dismissed as being not real. Not real PR, not serious, and you, by extension, are not a serious business-minded person. That has always pissed me off.*

2004 Starts first website *messycloset.net*

Crosby used this internal fire and her advisor's encouragement to fly to New York to interview some of the brightest minds in fashion PR. She wasn't able to find many online resources on fashion PR, so Crosby knew she'd have to go directly to them.

> **I thought, "I can build a space and resources that would help individuals succeed professionally." At the time, I didn't connect it but now I see where I was going with it all—there's a branding and presentation component to standing out and getting noticed.**

This thesis would later create the foundational principles of her fashion PR blog, *PR Couture*, but there's more to the story.

The PR Professional

Working in public relations gives you the opportunity to choose between working in-house, for an agency, or as a freelancer. Crosby, being the career-driven person she is, had experience in all three areas before deciding to take her blog full-time.

She first began working in-house for a jewelry company. Her job description included writing creative copy, naming jewelry lines and individual products, and media pitching.

After two years of working in-house, Crosby decided to pivot and work for an agency. She also started freelancing as an independent contractor with other agencies. This helped her get a crash course in freelancing, something she's still thankful for today.

The PR Blogger

It was during this time of new beginnings that Crosby gave herself the green light to create a fashion PR blog in 2006. *PR Couture* began as a way to educate others about the exciting field of fashion PR, but it was also created to help Crosby market herself for future job positions.

2004 Gets in to San Diego State communications graduate program   **2006** Starts *PR Couture*

Writing with the understanding voice of a mentor mixed with the encouragement of a best friend, Crosby quickly built the fashion PR resource she needed when she first began exploring the field in college.

> *I didn't create PR Couture with the intent of it being a full-blown business. My whole approach, and I think the approach that still comes out of today's version of the industry platform and sourcebook, is "We are 100 percent authentically here to fuel the field forward and support fashion and lifestyle communicators in every way we can—through highly-actionable content, expert insights, job leads, digital tools—you name it."*

Crosby was in the middle of a learning curve building *PR Couture*. On top of that, she also began working at a different agency to help with the launch of a women's store. While she learned a lot in the new position, it didn't last long.

> " **I didn't create *PR Couture* with the intent of it being a full-blown business.**

Crosby's mother passed away two weeks after the women's store launch. She traveled home for her mother's funeral to grieve with her family—and after two weeks away, she was let go from her position.

> *Looking back, that was the best thing ever because I needed to hang out on the couch for a while. I kept writing and working on the blog, and then a friend of mine referred me to an agency that had spontaneously decided that social media was something they should probably get into.*

Crosby went into this job interview different than any other interview in the past.

Knowing what was most important to her, she explained her depth of experience, what she wanted out the position, and even quoted a salary number $20,000 higher than her last role. If she was going to go back to agency life, it had to be for the right position and under the right circumstances.

Much to her surprise, they sent her a formal job offer matching her salary and conditions. She accepted, and over the next five years, she had the creative freedom to build the social media department from the ground up for one of the most well-run PR agencies that she's encountered. No micromanaging, no red tape, no walking on eggshells. It was the kind of work environment she had been dreaming about.

The top executives at the agency also loved that Crosby was building *PR Couture* on the side. She had several opportunities to speak at events on behalf of both her fashion PR blog and the agency.

During her time at the agency, she also wrote a book titled, *Ready to Launch: The PR Couture Guide to Breaking into Fashion PR* in 2012. Inspired largely by her blog

readers, she wanted to write a book that could act as their field guide to landing their own dream PR job.

In her last six months at the agency, she became the creative director of not only the social media department, but also their new content marketing arm. However, Crosby felt unenthusiastic about building a department from scratch again.

> *I kept thinking I've written a book, I have this whole business thing that's also happening, and I think this is just the time where I go and do that full-time.*

I'm Quitting

Before making the decision to quit, Crosby wanted to know she had her financial ducks in a row. After intentionally saving money she earned from book sales along with savings from her agency income, she gave herself a year to try full-time entrepreneurship.

Crosby began her journey into full-time business by editing the first version of her *Ready to Launch* book.

> *I was waking up at 6:00 in the morning full of energy, and I couldn't wait to get down to my computer and write. I would make coffee in the French press, put on a playlist, and sit at my yellow kitchen table to write all day. I would forget to eat or move, but I was so happy.*

Shortly after editing and re-publishing her book, she started teaching an in-person workshop, Fashion PR 101, with a partner and friend in the industry. She loved flying to New York for each workshop, but wanted to find a way to help a larger audience online.

Crosby was inspired to reimagine the in-person workshop curriculum and turn it into an online PR and career-growth course called Prism in 2015. Welcoming hundreds of students into the course and seeing them put the material into action—and securing top PR positions as a result—became a highlight of Crosby's career.

> "I was waking up at 6:00 in the morning full of energy, and I couldn't wait to get down to my computer and write.

The Business Today

As Crosby dreams up her newest offering, she's grateful for the small-but-mighty team that allows her to continually grow her blog and business.

Her team currently consists of an online business manager, part-time general strategist, and an intern from her alma mater of San Diego State. She also works in close collaboration with a design team and short-term volunteers from her Prism course who are looking for extra experience and a reference.

What started as a solo project has now grown into a tight-knit community of its own, helping the larger community of PR blog readers grow in their professional careers.

PR Couture has now grown into the number one fashion PR blog on the web—and shows no signs of stopping. Crosby has exceeded her previous executive-level agency salary with her business income—and she's seen firsthand just how influential the field of professional blogging has become.

> *When I look at the business now, a lot of what I do in my day-to-day job has less and less to do with the actual industry.*

> To know we've had an instrumental hand in actually building careers, fostering genuine relationships… that's unmatched, it's simply incredible.

Crosby has always been interested in redefining the public's view of fashion, public relations, and the relationship between the two industries. She's a box-breaker and risk-taker, relentlessly pursuing her vision in business and life.

After ten years with *PR Couture* in 2016, Crosby reflects on the successes and transitions she's made throughout her decade of blogging experience. The most memorable part of her career has been receiving kind messages from her readers over the years.

After reading an article that called her the "nice girl of fashion PR," she realized just how much of an impact she's had in this specialized industry.

> *There's been a whole generation where my book has been instrumental. They say, "It gave me the encouragement to actually move to New York, and now I'm the director of whatever," and I reply, "Oh my god." To know we've had an instrumental hand in actually building careers, fostering genuine relationships ... that's unmatched, it's simply incredible.*

From teaching a fashion PR class at San Diego State to receiving messages from those who attribute *PR Couture* to their success, everything about Crosby's story feels like a full circle moment.

She inspires us to think outside the box, exercise our creativity, and spend a little more time dressing up.

The Business Today

Revenue Breakdown

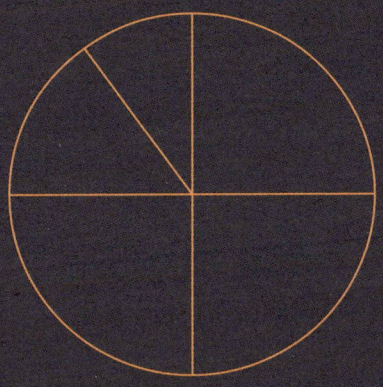

25% Online courses

25% Advertising

25% Products

15% Professional consulting

10% Affiliate sales

By the Numbers

75,000 Blog readers per month

16,000 Email subscribers

$50,000 Funds in the bank from book royalties and savings that allowed Crosby to quit her agency job

Products & Services

- PRISM online course
- *Ready to Launch* book
- *Pitch Perfect* eBook
- Digital templates for emails and pitches
- Consulting sessions
- PRISM Labs membership site (Coming soon)

Book Success

2,100+
Copies sold of *Ready to Launch: The PR Couture Guide to Breaking into Fashion PR*

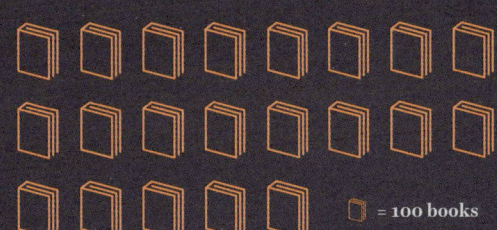

= 100 books

prcouture.com

Chad Collins

LEGO® Enthusiast. Family Man. Entrepreneur. Vlogger.

WORDS BY KAYLA HOLLATZ • PHOTOGRAPHY BY CALEB WOJCIK

As his group of friends tore into their new packs of baseball cards, Chad Collins watched closely. He bought a backpack full of those sealed packs at a recent baseball card show and brought them to recess with quite an industrious plan in mind for a third grader.

He sold those baseball card packs to his friends and if he saw one he knew was valuable as they opened their packs, he'd offer a trade—that one card for a whole new pack.

His friends got more cards of course, but Chad got all the value. This exchange rate worked well until the principal got word of that "business", and he was quickly shut down. But a business mindset had been born.

Chad's schoolyard side hustle is no surprise considering he grew up in a family of entrepreneurs. It's that quick-minded, entrepreneurial heart that would eventually lead Chad to create Brick Fest Live, a LEGO® Fan experience.

And while he knew the ups and downs of that entrepreneur lifestyle, as Chad grew up, he convinced himself that wasn't the life for him. So instead of giving into that entrepreneurial spirit early on, Chad began his adulthood seeking a more stable livelihood.

A LEGO®-Inspired Shift

Like many kids who play with LEGO®, Chad was inspired to turn his knack for building things into an engineering career. After some time at a global security and aerospace company, Chad eventually landed a job at a well-established startup. It was the perfect mix of stability and entrepreneurship.

But working in that fast-paced startup setting proved to be a less than optimal fit for Chad. He traveled a lot for work, which meant spending less time with his family. He was either flying to a new city for client meetings or commuting a total of three hours each day.

Since one of Chad's core values has always been spending quality time with his family, the job was beginning to put a huge strain on his life. But then everything changed with a simple lunch meeting.

One of Chad's friends invited him to lunch at a nearby mall, and while walking to the restaurant together, Chad spotted a LEGO® store.

Chad had no idea that LEGO® stores even existed, so Chad asked his friend if they could make a quick stop inside. At the back of the store, Chad saw a big wall where you could fill a cup with different LEGO® bricks instead of having to buy a full set.

Feeling like a kid again, Chad grabbed a cup and filled it to the brim with LEGO®. He brought his new collection home that night, much to his seven-year-old daughter Jordyn's delight.

As Jordyn's love for LEGO® grew, she started to search for inspiration videos on YouTube. One day, she asked Chad if they could create a YouTube channel together under the name Your Creative Friends. Through the channel, they could share their LEGO® creations and have an additional excuse to try out new LEGO® sets. Chad enthusiastically agreed, and they started planning their first video.

The very next day, he uploaded a quick video on how to fit more LEGO® bricks into their standard cup at the store. The video received over ten thousand views in the first couple of weeks.

As more people found their YouTube channel, their audience began asking when the next video was coming out. Chad took the video content more seriously, noticing there was a large amount of opportunity he could tap into with this passion project.

> *YouTube was everything for us, and really my daughter Jordyn was everything. If she didn't light that spark for LEGO®, and if she didn't request to create a YouTube channel, we wouldn't be in business today.*

2012 Creates first YouTube video with daughter Jordyn

What started as a way to bring Chad closer to his daughter and preserve his memories as a kid turned into a business. But before Chad could start his business, he put his focus on connecting with his YouTube audience.

Launching His First Event Experience

As Jordyn and Chad filmed and uploaded new YouTube videos, they were inspired to look for LEGO®-themed events they could attend together. Connecting with other LEGO® enthusiasts online was great, but it would be even better to meet them in person.

Chad began searching for events in the Philadelphia area, but there weren't any. The closest event he could find was several states away. That's when the lightbulb turned on.

> *I thought if there isn't an event like this in the Philadelphia market, and we have this YouTube audience of people now that we serve with our great content, then maybe they'll all come to the show that we produce.*

> **YouTube was everything for us, and really my daughter Jordyn was everything. If she didn't light that spark for LEGO®, and if she didn't request to create a YouTube channel, we wouldn't be in business today.**

Wanting to test his idea, he put early bird tickets on sale for their own event— an in-person LEGO®-inspired event experience, Brick Fest Live, that would happen several months later. It also helped that *The LEGO® Movie* had just been released in 2014, so the event was timely.

In the first weekend of his ticket presell campaign, over five thousand people bought tickets. The event was meant to be a side hustle, but it quickly seemed to have sustainable income potential.

In the next few months, they sold even more event tickets—for a grand total of thirteen thousand. After stopping ticket sales, Chad decided to have some tickets available at the door on the day of the event. He didn't expect that ten thousand more people would show up to buy same-day tickets because they weren't able to buy them online.

The first Brick Fest Live experience represented a lot for the Collins family, but the biggest question Chad now had to answer was when to take the leap from his full-time job. After so many hours of commuting and traveling over the years, working at home in his pajamas with his family nearby sounded like a perfect fit.

He was already making comparable income with the first event, so it motivated him to create a strategy for leaving the startup to pursue his own business.

After a few conversations with his wife in the fall, they decided that Chad should quit his day job in February, two months before their first event. That gave him enough time to put all of his attention into creating a great event, while also still providing additional financial security for his family for the new few months.

One day in December, Chad was driving to the office and received a text message about all the things he had on his schedule that week. Instead of responding to the text message, he called his wife and told her that he thought this was the day to leave.

After getting the thumbs-up from his wife, he found the CEO that day and put in his two weeks' notice. He admits that quitting his job before the first event had even happened was a little scary, but he knew he was onto something.

Pursuing Brick Fest Live Full-Time

With the success of the first live event, Chad was excited to put tickets on sale for the second show. And when that second show had the same amazing turnout as the first, Chad was filled with confidence to start hiring staff and investing in new attractions.

For the first two years, he invested all of the money they made back into the business to streamline their processes and come up with new attractions that would entice families to keep coming back.

Chad has always looked at Brick Fest Live as a family-focused experience rather than just a two-day event. He wanted to inspire parents and their kids to unleash their creativity and explore their imagination.

> *LEGO® is a timeless toy spanning generations. The LEGO® bricks that are made today are compatible with the LEGO® bricks that were made thirty years ago. They bring out memories in parents that they had when they were building with their parents. So they'll come to a show, and they're gonna have that same connection with their son or daughter that they had with their mother or father.*

The best reward of running Brick Fest Live is that it gives Chad more time to spend with his own family. Instead of taking long trips to work in his car, he takes trips to the toy store with his kids to pick up the latest LEGO® set so they can build something new and record a YouTube video afterward.

While his normal day can consist of anything from contract negotiations to brainstorming new attractions for each event, Chad knows that his family is always nearby. He now trades business flights for road trips with his family.

> *Instead of going on a business trip for eight days... now our family hits the road for thirty days to host three Brick Fest Live events. We also get to sightsee and have these amazing adventures with just the four of us that would be impossible to have otherwise.*

His family is integral to every aspect of his business. His wife greets attendees at the events, and his in-laws help with merchandise sales. His kids frequently appear in his YouTube videos and love participating in the events.

> " **Instead of going on a business trip for eight days now our family hits the road for thirty days to host three Brick Fest Live events.**

Building a talented team of employees has also helped Chad scale rather quickly while preserving his family time. With fifteen employees, he runs three large-scale event productions. In addition to Brick Fest Live, he and his business partner Gabe Young produce two other events: Minefaire, an official MINECRAFT community event, and Young Innovators Fair, a family Science and Tech Expo.

With a marketing, operations, and finance team working in alignment, they've been able to increase how many events they host each year. In 2016, they put on a total of fifteen events. A year later, they doubled that number to thirty.

> *The only way you can accomplish something is by having just a fantastic team that believes in the messaging of the company. Our mission is to provide a unique educational experience where families can come together and just have a blast.*

Taking a look behind the curtain of Chad's business, you'll see that, while ticket sales bring in the largest amount of revenue, there are many other income streams at play. Vendors pay to have space on the showroom floor—which creates a steady stream of income, much like event sponsors who want to have their name attached to the show.

2015 Business partner Gabe Young joins **2016** Hosts fifteen events **2017** Hosts thirty events

Merchandise sold at the events provides another source of revenue. They also have a membership box service that sends members LEGO®-themed merchandise every month. Affiliate marketing is one of their lower-tier revenue drivers but gives them the opportunity to monetize their video content.

Chad notes that the reason why they have been able to make changes and experiment with new income streams is because they've always had a strong audience. From his early days on YouTube, Chad has always prioritized conversations with his customers, attendees, and community members.

Looking back on the success of his business, Chad is thankful that his love for LEGO® and entrepreneurship was sparked at a young age. Instead of building someone else's dream as an engineer, he's now able to take those same skills and inject them into his business.

> *Building your business is for you and your legacy. It doesn't matter what you're doing . . . because you're not working; you're living. For us, we've created this blend with family and our lifestyle . . . where we have fun in our experiences every single day.*

Proving that LEGO® is for everyone to enjoy, Chad can frequently be found building new cities out of LEGO® bricks with his kids huddled around the kitchen table, hoping they carry on the family tradition and always make time for play.

The Business Today

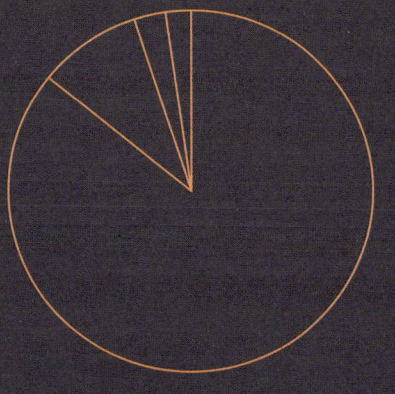

Revenue Breakdown

86% Ticket sales **9%** Vendor stands

3% Merchandise **2%** Sponsorships

Launch Success

23,000
Tickets sold for the first event

5,000 presales   8,000 online ticket sales   10,000 door sales at the event

By the Numbers

 12,246,756
Video views on YouTube

 412,000
Email subscribers

Products & Services

- Brick Fest Live LEGO® events
- Minefaire MINECRAFT events
- Young Innovators Fair expo
- Merchandise
- Monthly membership box

brickfestlive.com

Brooke Schoenman

Traveler. Dreamer. Entrepreneur. Creative. Minimalist. Blogger.

WORDS BY KAYLA HOLLATZ • PHOTOGRAPHY BY MARK FORBES

When asked what she wanted to be when she grew up, Brooke Schoenman answered "everything" with a hearty laugh. As a self-proclaimed dreamer, she has never wanted to pursue just one career path.

She remembers wanting to be an archeologist or paleontologist for a few years, but then she became fascinated with tracking weather patterns. The idea of chasing storms for a living seemed exciting so she dropped her plans to become an archaeologist in pursuit of something more adventurous. She also had an affinity for *The X-Files*, so—naturally—she also wanted to become a top FBI agent.

Her aspirations would come and go depending on the season, the unifying thread between them all was a deep need to explore new ideas and untouched terrain.

> *I feel like I still am the same way. I want to do everything. I still don't know what I want to be. I'm just always evolving, I guess.*

Brooke had no shortage of dream career paths, but it wasn't until she was a teenager that she decided to take a chance on one of her big ideas.

In 1999, Brooke was in an all-girl pop-grunge band that took her on a tour from her hometown in Central Illinois to Florida. Being pre-social media, setting this up was a huge feat. Brooke loved traveling with her bandmates on the road just as much as performing with them on stage each night.

During this month-long tour, Brooke and her band organized shows, recorded music, designed merch, and tracked sales and expenses. Brooke credits the band as her very first business but it wouldn't be her last.

Breaking Conventions at an Early Age

Born and raised in Peoria, a mid-size town in Illinois, Brooke always felt like an outlier in her family. No one in her family was passionate about traveling, but she couldn't shake the desire to explore every corner of the globe.

After taking Latin classes for four years in high school, she had the opportunity to follow her classmates to Italy when she was seventeen years old. This trip was outside the norm for Brooke's family; at that time, her mom had yet to go on an international trip and her father was afraid of flying. Even so, it only took a couple weeks in Italy for Brooke to know she would do anything to keep traveling.

Brooke's mom jokingly says she wishes she wouldn't have let Brooke go on her first international trip because then maybe Brooke would still live nearby instead of across the world.

After high school Brooke enrolled in the business school at the University of Illinois. However, it only took a few semesters for her to realize she didn't feel connected to the people in class or the subjects she was studying.

No one could understand why Brooke would intentionally give up her highly coveted spot at a top business school, but she was already used to going against the grain and trusting her instincts.

Wanting to study abroad and travel while she was in college, Brooke changed her major to international studies. It was a relatively new program at the time, so she had the freedom to pick and choose what classes she wanted to take.

In 2004, she had the opportunity to study abroad in Italy and revisit the scenery she fell in love with years ago. It was also the first time she would travel for a portion of

the trip on her own, staying in hostels and meeting people from different cultures. When she returned, she took on a whole new minimalist approach to travel and began to plan what it would take to travel long-term.

> *I came home from Italy, and I remember getting rid of so much stuff at home because . . . I didn't need it if I'm going to be leaving. I imagined a semester with just my suitcase. I remember feeling very excited about that.*

Seriously Saving up for Full-Time Travel

Even with this goal in mind, she didn't dive headfirst into full-time travel. Instead, she stayed in Illinois to work. Over a couple of years, Brooke took a job at a catering company as well as an IT position at Caterpillar. The corporate world would come with sacrifices, but if she could save up for a year of travel, it was worth it to Brooke.

During her time at Caterpillar, Brooke became an avid reader of travel blogs like *Me-Go* and connected with other travelers in travel-related online message boards. It only fueled her passion for full-time travel even more as she made friends who were living examples of what she wanted to do.

Knowing her mom was still unsure about Brooke's travel plans, she shared blog posts from other solo female travel bloggers to ease her mom into the idea. It took a couple of years for her mom to warm up to the idea but Brooke spent that time aggressively saving for her international trip.

By 2007, Brooke had saved enough money and was ready to quit her IT job.

This was the moment she had been preparing for. After years of working jobs she didn't love, she could now finally reward herself with a full year of international travel.

With most of her trip already mapped out, she booked a one-way ticket to Spain and packed a small suitcase. She couldn't wait to trade her apartment space and almost everything she owned to fulfill her childhood dream. She had never been so excited to jump into the unknown.

Brooke's Full Year of International Travel

Right before Brooke set out for her trip in 2007, she started a travel blog with a few affiliate links under the name *Brooke vs. the World*. At the time, she was treating it more like a personal diary than a travel resource.

Brooke kicked off her year of full-time travel by volunteering with a month-long archeological dig in Spain. There she met many other young people around her age who also dreamed about becoming archaeologists when they were kids. They spent the whole month uncovering an old Roman fort on a small island. It was the perfect way to start her year of travel.

Now that one of Brooke's childhood dreams had come true, she was excited to continue her trip to Central Asia. When choosing locations to visit, Brooke wanted to visit countries that offered many learning experiences, which led her to Kyrgyzstan.

> *I feel like if I'm not learning something, then I'm bored. I feel like I'm not living my life . . . and kind of wasting time. I just don't want to waste my life.*

While there, she enrolled in one-on-one Russian classes with native speakers for an extremely affordable price of four dollars an hour. She knew the best way to learn was to be immersed in the language so she spent hours a day practicing with her teachers. At the language school, she met many wonderful people she still stays in contact with today.

Even though Central Asia is not a tourist hotspot, it's one of Brooke's favorite places to visit because of its inclusive culture and the hospitality of the people who live there.

> **I feel like if I'm not learning something, then I'm bored. I feel like I'm not living my life and kind of wasting time. I just don't want to waste my life.**

Going Back to Full-Time Employment

After her stay in Central Asia and spending several weeks traveling Eastern Europe, Brooke saw her bank balance was getting smaller with no money coming in. After so many months of travel, it was time to find a more stable position where she could practice speaking Russian while saving more money for travel.

Brooke got a job teaching English in Ukraine around 2008 where she immediately bonded with her students, most of whom were young adults. And although she loved her students and charming society in Ukraine, the fall of the global economy forced her to consider leaving Ukraine. The global financial crisis affected the currency exchange rate at the time, meaning teachers like Brooke were making less money than they originally thought.

This put an immediate strain on her finances, which caused Brooke to take her blog more seriously than ever before.

> *I remember sitting in my room after lesson planning and blogging. Then I started submitting articles to other sites to make money. At that point, I just started thinking, "How can I make money online? How can I do this with my blog?"*

After working in Ukraine for five months, she followed a friend she met in Eastern Europe to Australia. With the financial strain in Ukraine behind her she received a working holiday visa and decided to relocate to Sydney in 2009. Australia has been her home base ever since.

In Sydney, Brooke worked with two companies helping them manage their blog and social media content. And as she looked for more freelance opportunities she started saving to travel again.

The Birth of *Her Packing List*

Brooke continued travel blogging on her personal website but felt the need to create more of a community around it. She didn't want it to just be a place to recount her own experiences through travel. She wanted to inspire other people to take the leap of faith into full-time travel and show them it wasn't as impossible as they may think.

During her time in Sydney, Brooke started a newsletter called *Female Travel Underground* which covered topics that were only relevant to solo women travelers. She remembers one of the first topics being about what kind of travel underwear to bring on a cross-country or international trip.

> *That is kind of how I got the inspiration for* Her Packing List *because I thought "This should be its own thing. It would be really easy for me to monetize with affiliate income and good information." That's basically how it was born in 2010.*

After transforming her newsletter content into her new website and travel resource, *Her Packing List*, she began promoting her content on social media and connecting more frequently with other travel bloggers.

While at a professional blogger conference in Melbourne, she checked into her blog traffic stats and saw a massive jump in pageviews. She went from 415 to 5,000 pageviews per day in just one month. Most of the traffic was coming from Pinterest and it continued to increase each month.

2008 Gets a teaching job in Ukraine

2009 Relocates to Sydney

It didn't take long before *Her Packing List* had more pageviews than Brooke's personal travel blog. What started as a simple side project had turned into a massive hit with travelers who wanted minimalist packing guides and travel advice.

In January 2013, Brooke noticed that she earned $360 through Amazon's affiliate program and that her blog had strong traffic. As her traffic continued to grow, she made plans to leave freelance writing in April so she could focus on scaling *Her Packing List* while also making Aroamas solid perfume sticks to market to her audience of travelers. This extra income provided her with more stability to take the leap later that year.

Now that she's working on *Her Packing List* full-time, she is thankful for the creative and location freedom it gives her. She's able to go to the gym and take an art class without any guilt because of how well the website is doing. It runs on its own while she prioritizes what truly matters to her: relationships and new learning experiences.

> You can be in the middle of nowhere, but if you meet awesome people, it's amazing. Maybe it's more unique when you meet them in really weird places.

A Real Look Into How Brooke Travels While Blogging

Although Brooke hasn't taken a long-term international trip in the last few years, she has still organized smaller trips to Malaysia and Germany, and she's gone back to the United States a few times to visit her family.

All of these trips have been supported by the income she's earned through *Her Packing List*. Brooke's business model is made up of equal parts advertisement

2010 Starts *Her Packing List* blog

2013 Stops freelancing to work on *Her Packing List* full-time

revenue and affiliate revenue. While she is more than comfortable with the income she's currently making with the blog, she's playing with different income streams to see which perform best.

Brooke's tried everything from creating eBooks to selling handmade solid perfume sticks. Her current projects include reformatting her eBook and reworking her course so she can launch it for the first time.

The most difficult part about scaling *Her Packing List* has been hiring the right help. Brooke doesn't enjoy managing people and likes to have her hands on different projects within the business. Luckily, she does have a blog contributor and blog manager who are helping her on a contract basis. Both of her freelancers love to travel too, so they deeply believe in the mission of *Her Packing List*.

Brooke attributes much of the success of *Her Packing List* to it being a very targeted and niche resource. The blog is for low-key travelers who are more interested in having the best cultural experience than learning how to pack fashionable things. Brooke doesn't wear makeup while she travels and doesn't worry about heels, so she has naturally attracted a blog audience that resonates with her travel style.

When asked what keeps her traveling after all this time, Brooke is quick to say it's the people who inspire her to explore new areas of the globe.

> *You can be in the middle of nowhere, but if you meet awesome people, it's amazing. Maybe it's more unique when you meet them in really weird places.*

2013 Launches Aroamas solid perfume sticks

Looking back at some of her favorite trips, she remembers a specific memory from her trip to Turkey that stands out from all the others. Brooke and her friends were staying with a local family in quaint rooms with big windows that led to the rooftop.

As Brooke stepped out onto the roof one morning, she saw a cluster of hot air balloons hovering ahead of her, painting the sky in every color imaginable. Watching them rise toward the clouds, she sipped her tea and let out a sigh of contentment.

Experiences like this have made the whole journey worth it.

The Business Today

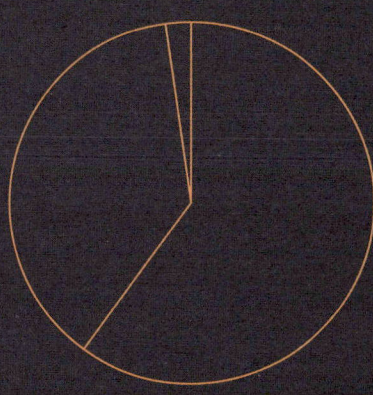

Revenue Breakdown

60% Advertising   **38%** Affiliate sales   **2%** Other

By the Numbers

310,800
Unique website visitors per month

387,500
Average sessions per month

12,800
Email subscribers

2
Contractors working with Brooke

Pageview Growth

SEPT 2012
415

OCT 2012
5,000

JAN 2013
8,500

APR 2018
606,600

herpackinglist.com

Corey Willis

Mother. Homemaker. Wife. Experimenter. Blogger.

WORDS BY KAYLA HOLLATZ • PHOTOGRAPHY BY KAMBRIA FISCHER

Corey Willis put her measuring tape on a nearby shelf after using it to draw faint pencil marks on the wall. She took a step back, taking in the full view of the blank canvas ahead of her.

Much to Corey's delight, she had been given full permission to turn her teen bedroom into her own personal sanctuary.

Picking up a paint brush, she carefully painted vibrantly colored bubbles. She topped off the look by incorporating the same primary colors into her two-way comforter.

It was one of the first decorating risks Corey had taken, but it wouldn't be her last.

In college, she gave new life to an old sofa that she found in a dumpster behind her apartment.

After recovering it, Corey headed to Walmart to buy inexpensive flat sheets. She planned to dye the sheets pink in the washing machine and use them as fabric to reupholster her "new" sofa. She got to work with the materials she had: sheets, upholstery tacks, and a hot glue gun. She figured out the rest as she went.

> *Once you gain the confidence of being able to think a project through and have it become something that's really beautiful and feels good in your home, it's kind of an addiction.*

Corey definitely sees things in a different way than most of us do. But long before she made a living teaching others how to decorate their homes, she was creating masterpieces purely for her own pleasure.

> "Once you gain the confidence of being able to think a project through and have it become something that's really beautiful and feels good in your home, it's kind of an addiction.

Growing Up

Corey's knack for creating a beautiful home on a budget has always been a part of her DNA. Living on a tight budget growing up in San Diego, Corey's parents instilled in her the value of creating a home. She was also taught that a little hard work, dedication, and innovative creativity could really stretch the decorating budget.

Corey credits much of her tenacity and DIY spirit to her parents. Corey's parents took a bit of a financial risk and bought a home in a great school district to raise her and her older brother. They may have had to survive on bean and cheese burritos and not having the latest and greatest gadgets and toys, but Corey reflects on her childhood with gratitude saying it was all worth it.

Living in San Diego, Corey was exposed to many Spanish-speaking students that became her close friends. They'd often come over to her house and spend time with Corey's family. She was fascinated by her friends' ability to learn the same school subjects she had to in their non-native language.

She convinced her parents to let her spend two summers abroad in Oaxaca, Mexico during her junior and senior year of high school. While there, she studied the language and lived with another family in a home with dirt floors, no electricity, and no running water.

This is where she became fluent in Spanish, and she went on to major in Spanish at San Diego State University immediately following her high school graduation.

Teaching With a Passion

After graduating from college, she spent the summer in Spain with some friends to experience the vibrant culture before moving to Santa Barbara to pursue a master's degree in education.

In Santa Barbara, she landed her first teaching job where she taught English as a second language (ESL) and first year Spanish.

> *I love dissecting language patterns in my own head and working backward to be able to explain why you don't say something in a certain way. But mostly, I love the people. There is so much hope, and immigrant students have a unique willingness to learn and pivot whenever they need to.*

During her first year teaching in Santa Barbara, she met her husband and married a few years later. Eventually they made the decision to relocate to San Diego to be near Corey's family.

During her first year teaching in Santa Barbara, she met her husband and married a few years later. When they got married, they made the decision to relocate to San Diego to be near Corey's family.

2003 Lands first teaching job

2008 Relocates to San Diego

Much to her disappointment, she was only able to find a job teaching Spanish classes in San Diego and missed the ESL community. She taught for two years in San Diego before becoming pregnant with her first child. And with that happy news, she paused her teaching career to become a stay-at-home mom.

When Corey's daughter was just a few weeks old, the family moved into a new house. It was a nice change from the cramped condo they lived in during her pregnancy. With a fresh, clean slate, Corey's mind raced with all the different things she could do to make this house feel like a true home.

Balancing Full-Time Motherhood With Blogging

Even after playing around with paint chips and giving some TLC to their house over the next few years, Corey still ached to do more. In the midst of her daily stay-at-home parent routine, she decided to start a blog just for fun.

She began mommy blogging under the name *Tiny Sidekick* where she published blog posts about arts and crafts projects she was doing with her kids.

Since her friends were always asking her for decorating tips, she decided to also share some of her style advice. As more people commented on her design blog posts, Corey realized that it should play a bigger role in her content strategy. Decorating on a budget had always been in her blood, so it felt like the perfect fit.

> I remember the day I made twelve cents from my blog, and I was like, "Holy shit, you can make money doing this? Game on."

Around this same time, Corey want to start earning money with her blog. She had more than a year's worth of free content in her blog archive, giving her a good foundation to test the waters of entrepreneurship.

2013 Starts *Tiny Sidekick* blog

2014 Started monetizing the blog

> *I remember the day I made twelve cents from my blog, and I was like, "Holy shit, you can make money doing this? Game on."*

She started monetizing with Google Adsense but was soon inspired to kick it up a notch. Her first big goal? She wanted to fully fund her kid's bathroom remodel with the money earned from her blog.

After reaching this goal, her confidence only continued to grow with each well received blog post and paycheck, knowing that she was helping people create a home they love.

In her first year of earning a living with her blog, she made $5,000 in side income. In her second year of monetization, her income grew to $35,000. She was determined to use her once "just for fun" passion project to help financially support her family and keep time with her kids and family at the top of her priority list.

A Life-Changing Rebrand

At the end of 2015, Corey faced one of the biggest decisions she would ever make in her business. Since she found herself writing more about home decor, she decided it would be best to rebrand under a different name.

She knew that having the term *DIY* in the name would be limiting and wouldn't allow her to talk about all forms of decorating. Corey felt that having the word *home* in the name would be important but wanted to pair it with something memorable. As she took a step back, she also realized that her friends often poked fun at her for greeting everyone with a simple *hey there!*

Taking the casual greeting, Corey pitched the new name, *Hey There, Home*, to a few close blog friends and her private Facebook group members, who she now lovingly calls "homies." Everyone mirrored her enthusiasm for the name.

When she started to reimagine the blog, Corey decided to hone in her messaging and share her heart behind decorating. The art of creating a welcoming, cozy, and livable home had never been a superficial practice for her. Decorating was important to her mother and her grandmother—and Corey intends to pass down the same passion for creating a home to her kids.

> *Anytime you're making a decor choice so that other people will think it's cool or pretty, it's the wrong choice. You can overthink it and then your house becomes a show home instead of a place to really live.*

Feeling like she had a good foundation to build from, Corey successfully rebranded and started immediately creating new content.

Investing in Her Craft

Using the same techniques she learned from creating lesson plans for the classroom, she turned her blog into a well-known resource for anyone looking to learn how to decorate, even if they don't think they have an eye for design.

> *I asked myself, "Is my blog content accessible? Could my cousin who has no clue about decorating do it if she wanted to?" With good instructions, readers can follow my decorating tips like a recipe. I can't make a fancy meal, but if I have a recipe, I can. It's the same idea.*

As Corey's blog traffic reached all new heights with her step-by-step tutorials and easy to follow decorating tips, she decided it was time to invest in her own business.

She bought a few online courses and had a great experience with mapping out her business goals through the *90 Day Year* program with Todd Herman. She still considers this to be one of her best investments to date.

Once she had learned enough through the courses to reach her next-level business goals, she focused her attention on finding the right people to help with her sales page copywriting and social media management.

Hiring for these tasks not only freed Corey to focus more of her time and attention on the things she preferred to be working on, but it also led to an increase in sales.

> " Anytime you're making a decor choice so that other people will think it's cool or pretty, it's the wrong choice. You can overthink it and then your house becomes a show home instead of a place to really live.

> I love waking up every day to see how much I made the day before. Earning $150 in ad revenue on days I just spent at the beach with my kids making sandcastles is a cool thing.

Her team helps her earn additional ad revenue by attracting more website traffic, and her copywriter has optimized conversion rates for her course sales page.

> *I love waking up every day to see how much I made the day before. Earning $150 in ad revenue on days I just spent at the beach with my kids making sandcastles is a cool thing.*

Corey's Business Model Today

After rebranding to *Hey There, Home*, Corey has transitioned to a more diversified business model. With multiple income streams, she's able to prioritize bigger projects that she's excited about while her team works on optimizing consistent revenue streams that already exist.

Corey currently has three main sources of income from her blog: ad revenue, digital products, and affiliate sales—with each making up about a third of the blog's total revenue.

The income stream she's most passionate about is her six-week online video course, Style Your Way Home. She crafted the course to help students not only discover what their unique style is, but also how to implement it within their own home.

The online course gives Corey the opportunity to revisit her teaching roots; she breaks down decorating concepts into easy to follow tips for her students in the video lessons and answers questions during live group calls.

As her blog continues to grow, Corey works about twenty hours every week while being a proud stay-at-home mom. She's reclaiming the often misunderstood title of homemaker and giving it a new definition we can all get behind.

A homemaker creates an environment and home that makes you feel creative. If you can walk in at the end of the day and know that, even if it's messy, everything has its place. It just feels good. It has to be your safe haven and your place to recharge. It has to reflect your personality and tell your story.

Corey is also working on writing new eBooks and creating additional courses. She admits to often juggling too many projects at a time, so she's thankful for her kids and supportive husband who help her stay true to her values.

Recently, her daughter came out to the garage while Corey was on her knees, drilling the last screws into her son's twin bed frame.

Her daughter asked, "Mom, why don't you just buy a bed? Why are you spending all this time in the garage building this thing?"

Corey saw this as an opportunity to share the core message of her work with her daughter, just like she's done with thousands of blog readers.

"Well," Corey said, "I'm building the bed because it's really fun to think of an idea, draw it out, think it through, and then do it to see if it can actually come to life."

Spoken like a true educator and entrepreneur.

The Business Today

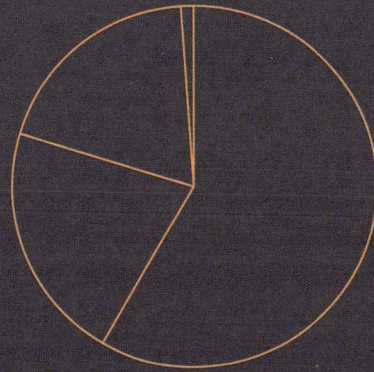

Revenue Breakdown

58% Advertising

21% Affiliate sales

19% Courses & digital products

1% Sponsored content

2013
Revenue from first year of blogging
$200

2014
Revenue from first year consciously monetizing
$5,000

2017
Annual revenue for *Hey There, Home*
$72,000

By the Numbers

 191,000
Unique visitors per month

 15,000
Email subscribers

 32%
Average newsletter open rate

Products & Services

- Style Your Way Home course
- #takebackmyspace Declutter Method workshop
- *10 Simple Sewing Projects for the Home* eBook
- Printable building and project plans

heytherehome.com

Asad Chaudhry

Magician. Entrepreneur. Teacher. YouTuber. Vlogger.

WORDS BY KAYLA HOLLATZ • PHOTOGRAPHY BY CALEB WOJCIK

Carefully opening his laptop, Asad Chaudhry logged into his Google AdSense account. He had done so every day this week and hoped to see his advertising income increase from yesterday's number.

He was used to his YouTube videos generating a dollar or two every few days, but today he noticed ten dollars of advertising revenue had been generated from his YouTube videos.

Beaming with pride, he quickly called his little brother to share the news. While ten dollars didn't seem to be a number worth getting excited about, it gave Asad a small taste of the earning potential behind his magic tricks.

Getting to do something he loved while generating passive income that day? He was living the dream.

The ten dollars I made through AdSense was more meaningful to me than making thousands of dollars at my engineering job because it was passive.

On a high from his first ten-dollar day, Asad began planning out his next month's video content while perfecting his sleight of hand technique.

No one else understood his passion for close-up magic, but Asad was determined to do something great with it.

Growing up in Colorado

Asad grew up in Colorado Springs with a fascination for collecting things. He started with rare stamps and coins, but later discovered his passion for playing basketball. This led him to collect basketball cards while also picking up a number of other hobbies in his early childhood.

> " The ten dollars I made through AdSense was more meaningful to me than making thousands of dollars at my engineering job because it was passive.

Asad's parents immigrated from Pakistan before he was born, but he remembers having a typical American childhood with his brothers. His dad came to America on an education scholarship and earned his PhD in engineering. Asad looked up to his hard-working, intelligent father and hoped to become like him one day.

Following in his footsteps, Asad considered a career in engineering—as did his two older brothers. Not knowing what he wanted to be when he grew up, engineering seemed to be a safe path.

While Asad doesn't remember the first time he thought about becoming an engineer, he does remember the pivotal moment that sparked his interest in magic.

An Early Love for Magic

In the early 2000s, most magicians were using big props on stage to pull off magic tricks. They focused more on distracting the audience's attention from the stunt than the actual trick itself.

It wasn't until Asad discovered David Blaine, a popular magician and street performer, that he became passionate about magic. David Blaine revolutionized magic with his close-up magic tricks using only a deck of cards. The world watched in awe and wonder as he made cards vanish with seamless technique.

Although Asad had seen magicians perform before, it was the first time he saw a magic trick and thought, *I want to do that*.

For the next few years, he became a sponge and read as many books on magic as he could find. YouTube wasn't available at the time so he wasn't able to find online tutorials. Instead, he practiced tricks in his bedroom and showed a few of them to his brothers.

But they didn't share Asad's passion for magic. After seeing a few of his magic tricks, they got sick of it. They did, however, perk up when Asad did a magic trick called The Coin Matrix.

To do the trick, you set four coins in four corners and cover each one with a card. When you complete the trick, the coins jump from all three cards and fall under one card.

It was such a powerful magic trick that it caught his doubtful brothers' attention. He still remembers their surprised reaction and how much they wanted him to reveal how he did it. To this day, Asad still hasn't shared that secret.

Even though his brothers never shared his love of magic, Asad's passion only grew as he got older.

> *My interest in magic has gone through a number of phases. You know, there'll be certain times when I'm just so into it, I can't drop a deck of cards I have in my hands. And then there were periods . . . where I had to focus on other aspects of life. But the passion always came back and came back stronger than before.*

Following in His Family's Footsteps

While Asad loved magic, he didn't think about pursuing it as a serious career in high school. But after a few semesters in college, Asad realized just how much hard work and dedication was involved to become an engineer. Knowing he needed a creative outlet after completing schoolwork, he turned to YouTube.

> *I would spend a lot of time on YouTube as a distraction from engineering school. I remember discovering that there are people making a living through YouTube by making videos and earning money through AdSense and online advertising. I thought that was such a cool way to make money. Once you put that video out, it continues to make money for you while you sleep. That struck me as a seriously cool thing.*

Before starting a YouTube channel of his own, he spent time watching videos from other popular video creators. Instead of watching TV, Asad watched vloggers on YouTube between classes.

> " **I remember discovering that there are people making a living through YouTube. I thought that was such a cool way to make money. Once you put that video out, it continues to make money for you while you sleep. That struck me as a seriously cool thing.**

Launching a YouTube Channel

After college, Asad landed a job as an engineer at RF Micro Devices in Greensboro, North Carolina. While he loved the people he worked with and the technological advancements, it still felt like a monotonous nine-to-five day job. To break up that monotony, Asad decided to launch his YouTube channel.

But before his launch, Asad entered a contest hosted by Mismag822, the most popular YouTube magician at the time. A couple times a year, Mismag822 would invite magicians of all skill levels to submit videos of innovative magic tricks.

Knowing he had nothing to lose, Asad uploaded a video he recorded of a trick he calls The Trick That Never Happened. It's a fairly long routine, but well worth the wait.

The cards are shown to be completely shuffled with the red cards and black cards randomly distributed throughout the pack. You openly separate the cards out so that you have a red pile and a black pile. A few quick tricks are performed with each pile, and at the end of the trick the deck is shown to once again be completely shuffled with the red and black cards randomly distributed throughout the whole pack.

While Asad now laughs at the poor quality of his flip camera recording, because of how well he presented the magic trick, he won the whole contest.

The prize was just a few decks of playing cards, but the real reward was seeing his YouTube subscriber count climb exponentially.

> *The contest got me started on YouTube. I had no idea where it would lead, but thinking back on it now, it's pretty crazy. If I hadn't entered that contest, I don't think I would have my own company right now.*

With considerable student loans to pay off, Asad decided it was time to start a passion project with magic that would allow him to generate some extra income on top of his engineering salary. Remembering that YouTube had been a good source of passive income for other video creators he followed, he decided to join YouTube in 2011.

After years of practicing magic in his childhood home and college dorm room, Asad finally had an opportunity to teach other people magic. Unlike his brothers, his YouTube subscribers weren't bored with his magic tricks. His audience couldn't wait to watch Asad's weekly tutorials, anxious to see what trick they would learn next.

He realized early on that other magicians on YouTube were uploading video tutorials that weren't well-produced or well-taught. But even though the videos were poor quality, they still received thousands of views—and sometimes millions of

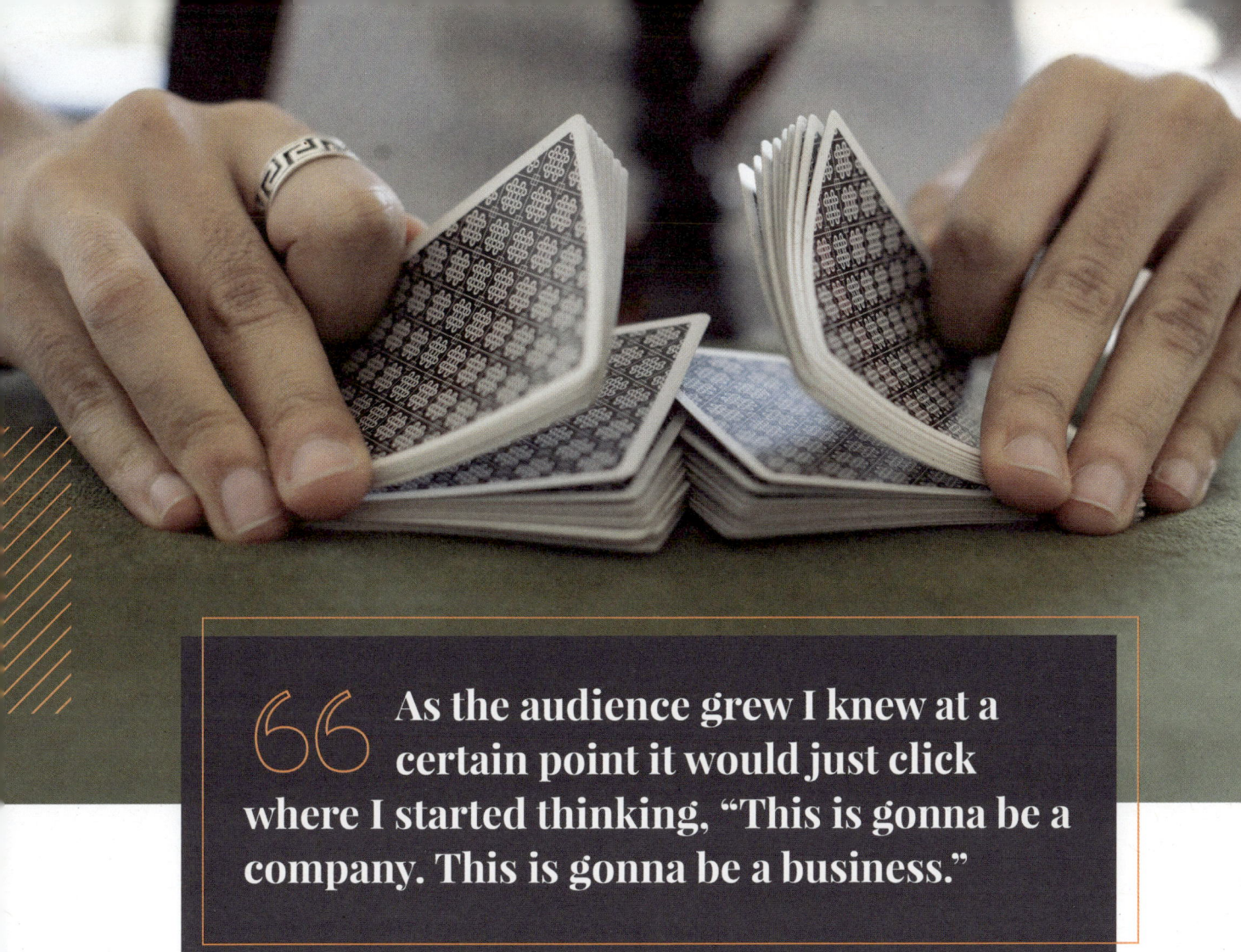

> **" As the audience grew I knew at a certain point it would just click where I started thinking, "This is gonna be a company. This is gonna be a business."**

views. Knowing he could create a better teaching experience, Asad set out to learn more about video production while putting his magic expertise into action.

During this time, Asad also relocated to Silicon Valley for his job. He wanted to live in California, so this opportunity came at the perfect time. Asad would come home from his engineering job and spend his whole evening creating videos for his YouTube channel.

> As the audience grew . . . I knew at a certain point it would just click where I started thinking, "This is gonna be a company. This is gonna be a business, and I'm going to be able to pivot from being an engineer to being a full-time YouTuber."

Becoming a Full-Time YouTuber

Asad grew his YouTube channel to 5,000 subscribers in his first year. And as he continued to publish weekly video tutorials, he saw his organic traffic spike. This led to more subscribers and more collaboration opportunities.

As his subscribers continued to grow, he saw the opportunity to create a larger strategy for his brand to stretch his YouTube channel into other platforms.

> *At the beginning, I was definitely focused only on YouTube, but I was aware of how important it is to have your own platform and to have your own home.*
>
> *I wanted a brand. I didn't want just a YouTube channel.*

To treat his YouTube channel more like a business, Asad built a companion website and rebranded his channel under the name *52Kards*. He also opened a community forum on his website while connecting with more followers through his Facebook page. In addition, Asad started his email list around this time but now says he wishes he would have started it sooner.

Once Asad hit the 100,000 YouTube subscriber mark, he noticed he could pay for most of his living expenses from his video ad revenue alone. His engineering job now took time away from growing his business rather than sustaining him while he grew it. Recognizing this pivotal shift, Asad quit his job to pursue *52Kards* full-time with a launch date in late 2014.

> *There's just a sense of fulfillment that comes with business. I think another part of the reason why I'm so interested in YouTube, in magic, and in this business is because it's also a great avenue for self-growth. I've learned so much in the process of doing all this, and I want to keep growing because I'm getting better at it.*

> "I wanted a brand. I didn't want just a YouTube channel."

Finding Success With Kickstarter

While most of his family and friends were a bit skeptical of Asad's decision to pursue his business full-time, he was motivated to transition fully into online education. His first big step was creating a Kickstarter project.

Instead of focusing on a physical product, Asad created a Kickstarter for an online course he wanted to create called Foundations of Card Magic. In the course, he planned to teach the most powerful card magic tricks he had learned in over ten years of experience. Because he already had a highly engaged audience on YouTube, he figured he might be able to hit his ambitious funding goal of $10,000.

To his surprise, he raised almost $70,000 at the end of the thirty-day period. Because it was a digital product, it was almost pure profit—and it sold even more copies after it was officially released.

Asad attributes much of his success to taking the alternative route to educating people on close-up magic tricks in an online format. Instead of having to flip through outdated books or watch DVDs, his course students can access lessons and tutorials from any device. It also provides Asad with a great profit margin.

Since his first Kickstarter was so successful, Asad plans to do at least one every year. It's his biggest promotion of the year, and he focuses the rest of his time on providing valuable free content on YouTube.

While $70,000 is an impressive amount to raise on Kickstarter, Asad raised even more funding for his MINT custom deck of luxury playing cards. After creating several digital products, Asad was inspired to try out the physical product income stream. He raised over $125,000 with 2,140 Kickstarter backers. A large portion of his revenue that year came from this campaign.

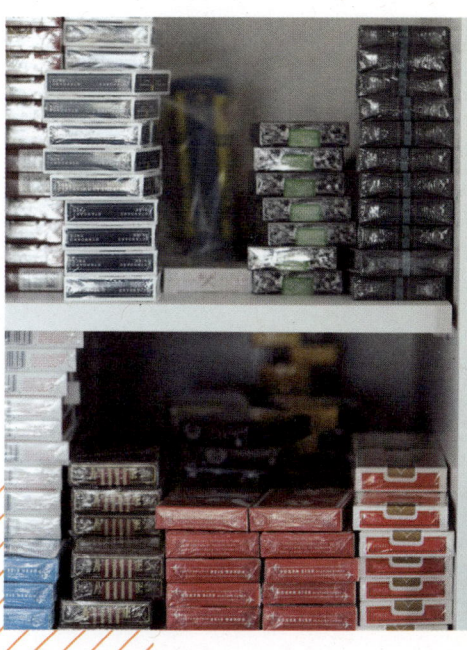

No End in Sight for *52Kards*

When asked to reflect on the success of his company, Asad can't help but remember his first deck of playing cards or his first viral video.

As one of the leading magic educators in the world, Asad focused on building diversified passive income streams that allow him to focus on creating great content for his audience of almost one million YouTube subscribers.

His most successful income stream, at around 60% of his income, is generated from his annual Kickstarter campaigns. Another 10% comes from YouTube advertising revenue, and 30% comes from his digital products and e-commerce shop, which is relatively new to *52Kards*.

His biggest struggle in expanding *52Kards* has been facing growing pains head-on. Adding more physical products to his offerings has complicated the order fulfillment process, but he loves having multiple income sources. While developing and selling physical products has been time-consuming, it's helped him better serve the loyal audience he's built on YouTube for over five years.

His favorite part of the business is still recording free educational videos for his subscribers, and all of his income streams intentionally fuel the helpful tutorials he creates on a weekly basis. He proudly considers himself not just a modern day magician but a vlogger too.

> *I would say being a creator means that you're taking your passions and expertise and then presenting it and distributing it to other people who are also interested in that subject. It's a great way to be able to express yourself.*

Asad didn't start his entrepreneurial journey knowing how to design a website, market his products on social media, or build an online community, but he's picked up all of these skills and more while consistently creating YouTube content.

He may not have known where his contest video would eventually lead him, but he's grateful that he's been able to turn his favorite hobby into a thriving career and business.

He's an example of what can be achieved when we mix curiosity and hard work with a little bit of beginner's luck.

The Business Today

Revenue Breakdown

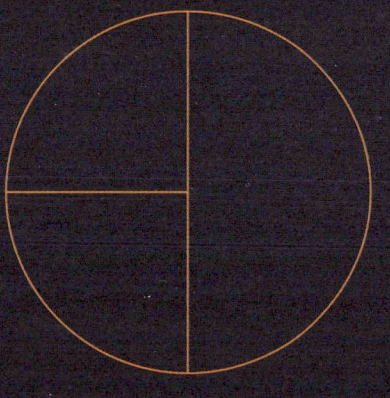

50% Physical products
25% Digital products
25% Advertising

By the Numbers

1,000,000
Video views per month

50,000
Email subscribers

Products & Services

- The Foundations of Card Magic course
- MINT Playing cards
- Free and paid courses
- Magic tricks and accessories

YouTube Subscriber Growth

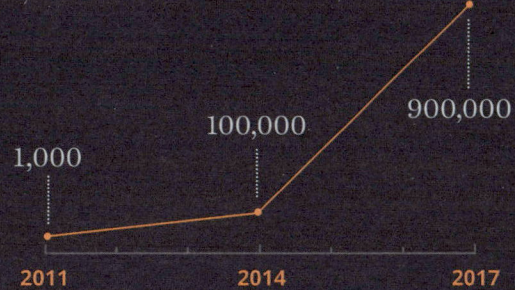

1,000 (2011) — 100,000 (2014) — 900,000 (2017)

Kickstarter Launches

2014 The Foundations of Card Magic
GOAL **$10,000** → RAISED **$70,000**

2016 MINT playing Cards
GOAL **$10,000** → RAISED **$125,000**

52kards.com

Krista Stryker

Athlete. Adventure Seeker. Writer. Entrepreneur. Blogger.

WORDS BY KAYLA HOLLATZ • PHOTOGRAPHY BY CALEB WOJCIK

Staring at the metal bar above her, Krista Stryker stretched her hands before grabbing on. For years, Krista's inner critic told her that she couldn't do a proper pull-up because her arms were too long and she wasn't strong enough.

After strengthening her arms for a few months, she found herself at the metal bar again. With a wide, tightened grip, she pulled her body upward so that her chin passed the bar before lowering herself toward the ground.

She did it. She had finally silenced her inner critic and eliminated the word impossible from her vocabulary with a single pull-up.

Shortly after reaching this goal, she focused on a new objective. Krista had always wanted to do a pistol squat—a one-legged squat where balance and strength are equally important. And once she had completed that goal, she was on to the next one.

While Krista had been involved in many sports at a young age, she started to consider herself a true athlete after training in Amsterdam and New York City.

> *Training really made me feel like I could do anything. It was kind of addicting. Once I got one skill, I wanted to do the harder version. It definitely became more about building strength than my looks.*

This renewed passion for strength training helped Krista embark on a fitness journey that would soon lead to a new career path. But before that could happen, she needed to discover what she didn't want to do for a living.

Big Dreams in a Small Town

Krista grew up in the small town of Camas, Washington, located just outside of Portland, Oregon. She learned a lot about entrepreneurship from her parents at a young age. Her dad was a dentist, and her mom, who once worked as a teacher, eventually took on the business manager role for the dentistry office.

Living in a small town, however, was difficult for an out-of-the-box thinker like Krista. In her spare time, she found herself lost in fictional worlds as the books she read offered the exciting adventures her small town couldn't provide.

Knowing adventure was important to her, Krista's parents always found time to play together and go on vacations. Balancing family life with the daily operations of running a successful dentistry business seemed to come naturally to her parents.

Krista admired what her parents did for a living, but she didn't grow up wanting to be a dentist or a business manager. Instead, she tried on many career aspirations to see what would feel like the right fit, but she couldn't find a single career path she wanted to stick with.

It didn't help that the small town she grew up in discouraged kids from pursuing their own thing. To appease her neighbors and teachers, Krista would have to follow a traditional academic path—but she went for a more unconventional route instead.

With the support of her parents, she left high school early to get her GED.

> *I hated high school. I remember telling my mom that I didn't want to learn anything ever again, but what I really know now is that I didn't want to be told what to learn.*

After feeling trapped for years, Krista finally felt like she could explore who she was outside of the small town when she enrolled in college at seventeen years old.

> **"Training really made me feel like I could do anything. It was kind of addicting. Once I got one skill, I wanted to do the harder version.**

Non-traditional College and Career Paths

In high school, Krista was inspired by photography and the ability to capture images from behind the lens. Struggling with her own identity, it felt like a safe career path and one where she didn't need to be on display.

She enrolled in a photography college in Santa Barbara, but only stayed there for nine months before deciding to transfer universities when she realized photography wasn't the only passion she wanted to pursue.

In total, Krista would attend five colleges before graduating with an international relations degree in just three and a half years. During college, Krista also noticed that she wasn't prioritizing her fitness and health.

She never felt exceptionally strong when she was growing up, but her non-active teenage years were catching up with her. At the time, Krista wasn't eating well and didn't have enough energy to sustain her throughout the day. More importantly, she noticed that her inactivity continued to affect her confidence.

> *I didn't feel very good in college. If you don't eat very well, it affects everything. It affects your mood and how well you think. And I didn't like how I looked. When you're seventeen or eighteen in college, that sucks. No one likes to feel insecure about their appearance.*

It was time for a change. Krista experimented with different kinds of exercise—things like running, weight lifting, and triathlon training.

While continuing to prioritize her health after graduation, Krista hoped to get a job at a local NPR station she previously interned at. She was interested in journalism and thought the entry-level position might get her foot in the door for bigger assignments, but the job market was at a record low.

2004 Enrolls in college at seventeen years old

After a few months of applying and interviewing for positions she didn't get, Krista decided to travel and live overseas for awhile. Her now-husband Brian transferred to Nike's Amsterdam office and they relocated together.

Krista envisioned becoming a journalist in Amsterdam because she thought they needed native English speakers. However, after a year and a half of waiting, she finally got her work visa but was turned down multiple times for journalist positions because she couldn't speak Dutch.

She did, however, start a travel blog. It was mainly written to update family and friends about their overseas adventures, but it only lasted a couple years. Krista never thought about monetizing it or making it her career.

Krista's true turning point was when she began working with a personal trainer in Amsterdam. After reaching her pull-up and pistol-squat goals, Krista dreamed about what it would be like to help other people with their own fitness journey.

> **When I could do something in the gym, it gave me a boost of confidence. I'd always thought this stuff was impossible so when I could do a pull-up, I thought "Well, maybe I can start a business."**

> *When I could do something in the gym, it gave me a boost of confidence. I'd always thought this stuff was impossible . . . so when I could do a pull-up, I thought, "Well, maybe I can start a business." It just opened up a lot of possibility for me. That's what I love about fitness; it can really change you.*

This inspired her to become a certified personal trainer in 2010, but by the time she received her certification, she was ready for a new beginning. She and Brian moved to New York for the next chapter of her career.

Designing Her Own Career

After moving back to the United States, Krista began working in a gym as a one-on-one personal trainer in 2011. While she liked the work itself, the job gave her little freedom.

The hours were difficult. Krista began her day meeting morning clients at 5:00 a.m., then had a big break in the middle of the day before she could meet with her evening clients around 6:00 p.m. It was exhausting, and she didn't want the gym to be in control of her schedule.

> *One of the things that I figured out from these various jobs was that I really hated working for other people. I really like having my own schedule. I didn't want to be in an office and waste time.*

It wasn't long before Krista began looking outside of personal training for a solution. She started reading business books like *The Hundred Dollar Startup* and *The 4-Hour Workweek*, and she spent her time browsing through blogs like

Copyblogger to learn how to become a freelance copywriter. She also took a course on copywriting to retrain herself on how to write in a specific style.

It was also during this time that she started a second blog with a focus on sharing personal development tips. She loved blogging and writing but didn't yet know how to turn it into a business.

A consultation call with Jon Morrow, a writer she admired from *Copyblogger*, confirmed that the blog centered on personal development tips wasn't a viable business idea. He affirmed that Krista was a great writer but that her efforts would be better directed toward a new project.

Krista wanted to create something bigger than herself, which then gave birth to a new blog and her first income stream.

Building a Fitness App

At the same time that she decided to blog under the brand name *12 Minute Athlete*, Krista thought about creating an app for blog readers who wanted quality exercise routines that they could fit into their busy schedule.

There weren't many fitness apps on the market in 2012, and of the apps that were available, most of them didn't provide workouts or additional support. Krista set out to create a unique app that would combine her personal training experience with her blog niche.

Much of the content had already been created through guiding her personal training clients in many high intensity interval training (HIIT) workouts. The only thing left to do was to find a developer.

Since Krista's husband is a designer, she collaborated with him on the wireframe design for the app. The wireframes showed a visual layout for how each app screen would look and function. Completing this step made it easier to find the right developer.

As the developer worked on the app, Krista continued to pick up freelance copywriting positions while blogging to sustain her audience growth. She knew she didn't want to be a lifelong copywriter, and Krista knew the app would be a great step forward.

Krista then focused her attention on launch marketing. She knew that to have a successful business, people had to know about what you were creating and get excited to share the app with their friends.

Although she was juggling multiple projects at a time, Krista worked intentionally on each one. This allowed her to work diligently without feeling the financial pressure to make the app her sole income generator too soon.

> *If you go slowly and test as you go, and you still have income, there's less pressure. And I think you're going to end up making something that's a better product or whatever you're trying to make in the end.*
>
> *I didn't even try to make money from my blog for six months. I just wanted to do the app, test it, and see if anyone resonated with what I was saying. And if people really didn't, I would have changed what I was doing, but I got enough of a response that I was encouraged to keep going.*

After launching the 12 Minute Athlete app, Krista saw several doors of opportunity fly open as she began testing more income streams. This allowed her to take a step back from freelance copywriting and personal training to pursue *12 Minute Athlete* full-time.

Krista's Business Today

Although the 12 Minute Athlete app may look like an overnight success to an outsider, it's taken years of hard work and self-discovery to grow the brand to where it is today.

Krista attributes much of its growth to the word-of-mouth recommendations from her loyal blog readers and app users. She always thought business success was about having a big break, but she now realizes it's the gradual process of building a brand you believe in and one you can stick with.

Blogging has given her an incredible amount of freedom, allowing her to work during her most productive hours of the day. She loves waking up in the morning and listening to NPR before she works for an hour. Then she takes her dog, Rocket, out for a walk around the neighborhood and does a couple hours of work at a nearby coffee shop before fitting in her workout.

Even though Krista has a great routine at home, she likes to switch it up every so often when she travels to new places.

> *Blogging has given me so much freedom. I can literally work from everywhere. My husband and I spent an entire month in Thailand and I worked every day, went swimming, and explored the markets. It was so fun.*

Not only does she have schedule freedom, but she also has newfound financial freedom. She has earned more income through *12 Minute Athlete* than any of her past salaries. This is much in thanks to her diversified business model.

Her 12 Minute Athlete app brings in around 30% of her total business income—with workout programs producing another 30% through eBook and online course sales. Influencer marketing has also created an extra lift, bringing in 10–15% of her total

> "Blogging has given me so much freedom. I can literally work from everywhere.

income depending on the season. December and January are usually her busiest months for influencer marketing campaigns because of the holidays and New Year's resolution themes. Affiliate and advertising income make up a small percentage too.

Even with multiple income streams already in place, she intends to scale her business into new channels in the next few years. She once read that a successful modern-day entrepreneur should have at least seven streams of income, so Krista continues to work toward that goal.

Now Krista treats every new business goal like her first fitness goals in Amsterdam: she proves that what seems impossible in the moment can be accomplished with dedication, tenacity, and guts.

The Business Today

Revenue Breakdown

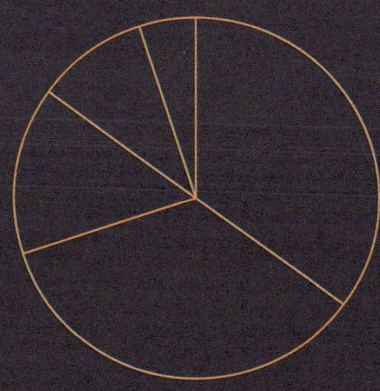

35% Apps

35% Workout programs

15% Influencer marketing

10% Affiliate sales

5% Advertising

By the Numbers

 300,000
Blog readers per month

 32,000
Email subscribers

Products & Services

- 12 Minute Athlete iPhone & Android apps
- Fitter Faster Stronger 2.0 90-day workout program
- Bodyweight Strength + Power Calisthenics workout program
- Pull Up Mastery skill-based program
- Rock the Pistol skill-based program
- Beginner Handstands skill-based program
- *Fight-Ready HIIT Workouts* eBook

App Downloads

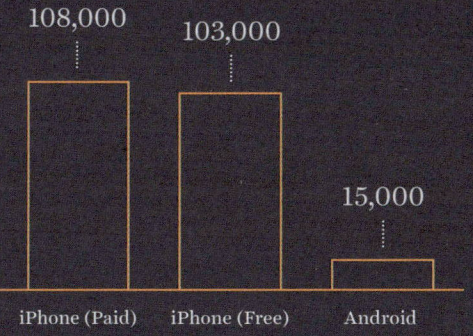

108,000 — iPhone (Paid)
103,000 — iPhone (Free)
15,000 — Android

12minuteathlete.com

Vanessa Levin

Teacher. Wife. Lifelong Learner. Blogger.

WORDS BY KAYLA HOLLATZ • PHOTOGRAPHY BY YESENIA AND JOSHUA FORTUNA

Sitting quietly at her school desk, Vanessa Levin took a sharpened pencil out of her backpack and looked at her fourth-grade teacher pacing in front of the classroom. A bulleted list of book titles was written on the chalkboard behind Miss Melon.

With a smile, Miss Melon began to pass out sheets of paper with a list of assignments. To Vanessa's surprise, she was able to choose what project she wanted to create for each book they read in class. You could earn full credit by creating a skit, writing a paper, or creating a piece of artwork.

Vanessa wasn't interested in assignments that required her to perform in front of the class, but she loved the idea of spending a week creating a shoebox diorama. She used all kinds of materials—from paint to clay to glitter.

Miss Melon approached teaching from a different perspective than other educators in the 1970s. By giving her students more creative freedom, Miss Melon left a

lasting impression on students like Vanessa. She inspired Vanessa to fully embrace nontraditional teaching methods in her own pre-K classroom decades later that would make her blog, *Pre-K Pages*, an in-demand teacher resource.

Lifelong Learner

Vanessa grew up in a traditional household in a small, rural town outside of Detroit. Everyone in her family line had worked in the automotive industry, which offered job security despite the hard, laborious work it required.

Vanessa, however, always had her sights set on being a teacher.

> *I always knew I wanted to be a teacher. That was always my game plan. I just loved school and learning. Laura Ingalls Wilder was my idol.*

Although her parents and extended family members hadn't gone to college, they were supportive of her career aspirations because becoming a teacher was also seen as a stable, practical career choice.

The following spring semester she was enrolled in Michigan State University in the education program. Choosing her major was easy but figuring out how to fund her tuition was not. Once she applied and received some grants, Vanessa's dream was finally possible and she packed her bags for Ann Arbor.

Becoming a Teacher

When it was time to put her degree to work, Vanessa realized that all of her friends had failed to find teaching positions after graduation. The job market was at an all-time low, meaning Vanessa had to find opportunities in other areas.

1992 Takes a teaching position in South Korea

1999 Moves to Dallas

She refused to be discouraged and took a teaching position overseas in Seoul, South Korea in 1992. Vanessa remembers her parents being somewhat terrified of her moving to an unknown place across the ocean, but she was excited to have a well-paying job and to set off on a new adventure.

> *I went over to South Korea and fell in love with it. I had a more global view after that. I just really wanted to help families who were trying to navigate this tricky thing we call English in America. When I came back to the States, I wanted to work not with just little kids, but also little kids who spoke English as a second language.*

After returning to America and teaching in Detroit for a year, Vanessa moved to Texas—a state growing at such a rapid rate that their school system had a desperate need for early childhood teachers.

It was in Houston that Vanessa met her husband. The following year they were married, moved to Dallas in 1999, and have been there ever since.

The Birth of Her Blog

In 2001, Vanessa's school district required teachers to create a website for their class, despite their lack of training materials on how to start a website. She couldn't believe no one could tell her how to do something that was now a mandatory part of the job. Undeterred, Vanessa spent the following summer creating a website using a platform called FrontPage.

She blogged under the name *Pre-K Pages* and became one of the pioneers in the pre-K blogging space. Since there weren't many preschool teachers blogging at the time, she was able to quickly grow her influence on Google.

This came in handy around 2006 when The Pew Charitable Trusts did a Google search for preschool teachers to help them create persuasive blog content around a platform issue during an upcoming election. Vanessa's blog was one of the top results.

After receiving an email from the organization, Vanessa couldn't believe out of all the preschool teachers in America, she was chosen to collaborate with this influential foundation. Somehow the blog that started as an educator requirement had turned into her greatest opportunity.

Vanessa wrote blog posts for the organization every month for a year along with other pre-K teacher contributors around the country. This guest blog-posting opportunity was instrumental in helping her gain credibility in her field.

Even though the blog had provided her with life-changing opportunities, Vanessa was still aware of the stigma around blogging at the time. Most people thought bloggers just sat around all day and talked about what they ate. She would often joke around with her friend, who was a fellow blogger, about what blogging even was.

> *In our eyes, we saw bloggers as people who were full of themselves, wanting to share pictures of their kids and what they had for breakfast. Then I did guest blogging with The Pew Charitable Trusts and I felt like, "Yeah, but then there's this kind of blog."*

Vanessa was committed to taking a different approach with her website. She didn't want it to be all about herself but rather a helpful resource for other preschool teachers. Even with her success, she never saw it as a business until her audience told her that she was sitting on a great business idea.

The Birth of Her Business

After providing her readers with free content for years, Vanessa noticed how often they were asking for more lesson plans. She received at least ten emails each day from teachers who wanted her to send them PDF attachments of her work.

It wasn't long before she could hardly keep up with the requests as they rolled in. One reader said she would be willing to pay her for the lesson plans but Vanessa felt weird about selling them. Her audience had to wear her down before a light bulb went off.

At first, Vanessa started with a downloadable report card and assessment tool priced at eight dollars. Nothing existed like this at the time, so they sold really well. She didn't sell advertisement space on her blog right away, but she did earn considerable income as an early Amazon affiliate.

But it wasn't until 2010 when she moved her website from FrontPage to WordPress that her business really picked up. She remembers the website taking off after that, which also had a lot to do with her Facebook page growth.

> *The traffic on the site was increasing, and the sales were increasing so I said, "I wonder, this might be crazy, but maybe I could make $50 a day." That was my big goal . . . because at the time, if you looked at my pay as a teacher, that's how much I would take home after taxes and insurance was taken out.*

> **"The traffic on the site was increasing, and the sales were increasing so I said, "I wonder, this might be crazy, but maybe I could make $50 a day." That was my big goal because at the time, if you looked at my pay as a teacher, that's how much I would take home.**

After selling many of her PDF products and gaining credibility with The Pew Charitable Trusts, she also received requests to professionally speak to other early childhood teachers. Speaking provided a great source of side income, and Vanessa quickly realized she could easily make more than she was teaching with her blog and speaking gigs.

Deciding to Pursue Blogging Full-Time

Before she thought about leaving her full-time teaching job, she set a goal to save at least one year's worth of her teaching salary. She talked with her husband about the goal and he was on board with her plan. By the end of the school year, she saved even more than what she earned through her teaching salary.

Faced with one of the biggest decisions of her life, Vanessa questioned whether she really wanted to leave the classroom. It seemed great in theory but now that the opportunity was actually here, she wasn't sure what the right choice would be. Her identity had been intimately tied to being a pre-K teacher for so long that it was hard to let go.

Vanessa didn't feel like she knew enough about the business side of running her blog, but she also knew it wouldn't have a chance to grow if she was tied to her full-time teaching job. She needed more time to create digital products to scale her business while taking speaking gigs.

Seeing the income her blog had already generated for her family, she decided to take the leap in July 2010. Even though she had a difficult time leaving her position, she knew her business would give her the opportunity to help even more preschool teachers make an impact in their own classrooms. As she settled into her new routine, she found that her biggest challenge was hiring the right team members to help with her blog growth.

> *When I started having to hire people, that was really hard because as teachers we're used to working on our own in our own classroom. We're in charge.*

As she learned to let go of projects, she was introduced to Jeni Elliott of *Biz Mavens* and began working with her in 2012 on the "business side" of blogging. Together, they created a game plan to help Vanessa scale her business to where it is today.

How Vanessa's Business Runs Today

Vanessa has tested dozens of income streams over the years—everything from affiliate programs and digital products to advertising space and speaking gigs.

By giving herself time and creative freedom to experiment with each income stream, she's built a sustainable business model that allows her to expand every year. It's so sustainable, in fact, that her husband quit his full-time job to work on *Pre-K Pages* in 2015.

> When I started having to hire people, that was really hard because as teachers we're used to working on our own in our own classroom. We're in charge.

> "You can start a blog in ten minutes. You can put ads on it, and you can be an Amazon affiliate. There's so many ways to monetize today that I think the minute that you start a blog, you're a business owner.

Vanessa is very transparent about her business model as a successful full-time blogger. Most of her income comes from a membership community, the *Teaching Tribe*, for pre-K teachers who are looking for additional resources. She has grown it to 2,000 members over the last few years.

She calls the *Teaching Tribe* "a safe haven for asking and answering questions for new and veteran teachers." That's a mission we can all get behind.

Inside the membership, her full library of 300+ products is available for download, along with new monthly two-hour trainings recorded through video. All of her products are still available for individual purchase in her shop, which generates some extra revenue as well.

Because her membership community is a recurring monthly revenue source, it's given Vanessa the freedom to pursue other creative projects while intentionally declining opportunities that don't feel like a perfect fit—like taking a step back from speaking to focus on the other areas of her blog.

Even with all of the success she's found with her blog since its inception in 2002, she still has difficulty explaining what she does.

> *People ask, "What do you do?" and I stumble around because I don't have time if I'm in an elevator pitch to explain to people what a blog is, so I usually say I'm an educational consultant. Then my husband says, "That's not truthful," and I say, "Well, I do train and consult with school districts and teachers." He says, "No. You need to tell them that you're a blogger, and you need to raise awareness of this." I would, but maybe I can just give them this coffee table book now.*

2015 Vanessa's husband joins her in working on *Pre-K Pages* full-time

There's no doubt that Vanessa is a trailblazing blogger. After over seventeen years of blogging, Vanessa still believes there's no better time to be a blogger than right now.

> *You can start a blog in ten minutes. You can put ads on it, and you can be an Amazon affiliate. There's so many ways to monetize today that I think the minute that you start a blog, you're a business owner.*

Everyone who meets Vanessa and hears her story walks away with a renewed passion for finding their own purpose. Perhaps it will lead them to start a blog of their own.

Miss Melon would be proud.

The Business Today

Revenue Breakdown

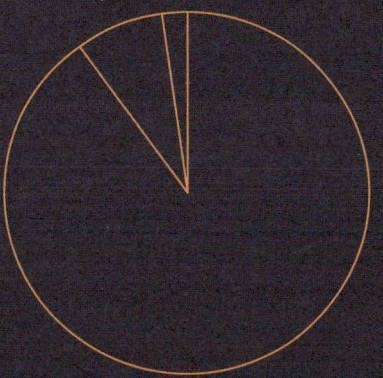

90% Membership site

8% Consulting/workshops

2% Affiliate sales

2010
Annual salary as a pre-K teacher
$54,000

2011
Revenue from first year working on *Pre-K Pages* full time
$65,000

2017
Current annual revenue from *Pre-K Pages*
$750,000

By the Numbers

750,000
Blog readers per month

 50,000
Email subscribers

2,000
Members in *The Teaching Tribe*

Products & Services

- *The Teaching Tribe* membership site
- Lesson plans and PDFs
- Online workshops
- Public speaking
- Consulting

pre-kpages.com

Dave Stuart Jr.

Teacher. Husband. Father. Writer. Speaker. Blogger.

WORDS BY KAYLA HOLLATZ • PHOTOGRAPHY BY CALEB WOJCIK

hen Dave opened the email, his pulse quickened. He had been waiting for this one. As he began reading, he pumped his fist in the air, elated.

He quickly reached for the phone to call his wife, Crystal.

> Honey, you know that rug we've been needing for the living room? We can get that now; we just earned some money from the blog.

He could feel his wife's joy through the phone.

A simple advertising sponsor email to his alma mater's marketing department had just earned Dave an extra $1800 in income from his six-month-old blog. As a full-time teacher with a modest salary, this was money that would help his family pay for items in their new home.

Later that afternoon as Dave helped Crystal unload the rug from her car, they both looked at each other with delight and disbelief.

Could it be that he had found a way to provide for his family while continuing to make an impact in the classroom as a high school teacher? This advertising contract was the first spark on Dave's blogging journey, but his story began long before he published his first blog post in May 2012.

Dave's Early Career Aspirations

As a kid, Dave had dreamed about becoming a writer. As an adolescent, however, he started to hear the concern in adult voices when they'd question him on these aspirations:

> *How much money do writers make? How do you ensure that you get a job doing that?*

Dave heeded those doubts, deciding instead to head to college as a pre-med major.

In college, Dave quickly realized that medicine wasn't for him. There was one particularly poignant experience where, as a freshman undergraduate, he shadowed a doctor. At the end of the shadowing experience, the doctor looked Dave in the eyes and said:

> *You had better love what you just saw because it will be your life.*

At about the same time, Dave started feeling the urge to work with young people. In his pre-med classes, he found himself daydreaming about teaching English and history during the school months and following his dream of being a writer during his summers off. Before long, Dave applied to the School of Education.

Dave had always been passionate about history, English, and education. He was inspired by his teachers throughout grade school and thought maybe becoming a teacher was his next best step. As he began studying education and student teaching, he knew he had found the right career path for him.

> *Teaching matters because all of human history is built on teaching. It's this constant investment in those who follow. Teaching in the classroom matters a lot to me because it's my calling, and I feel like I'm just made to teach these kids about world history and life.*

He graduated a few years later with his bachelor's degree in education.

Becoming a Teacher—And an Eternal Student

In 2006, Dave began his teaching career in Baltimore, Maryland, where he taught English Language Arts to middle schoolers. A couple of years later, he married his wife, Crystal, and, after spending a year in New York City together while Crystal finished her undergraduate degree, the couple moved to their home state of Michigan in 2010.

> **Teaching matters because all of human history is built on teaching. It's this constant investment in those who follow.**

During their first few months back in the state, Dave tried (and failed) to find a full-time teaching position. It was a humbling season of life, as Dave had expected that his three years teaching in Baltimore would make him an appealing candidate to hiring committees.

Ultimately, Dave was thankful to land a long-term substitute teaching position in Cedar Springs. This paid the bills, but barely—especially considering the addition of their first child, Haddie, in 2010. The family was grateful to get by living on $75 a day, thanks to the generosity of others and the help of a government assistance program for mothers and children.

> "I'm very thankful that I had a paycheck that could provide for my family during that time because I think it was the key to immersing myself in the different ways you can earn income through an online business.

It was during this time period that Dave reached out to a mentor of his in New York City, Tim Knapp. Tim had once been a teacher in Oklahoma, and to help provide for his family, Tim had worked various side hustles until finally landing on the entrepreneurial venture that he ultimately switched to from teaching. Dave had no desire to leave teaching, but he did want more financial security for his family. Tim encouraged Dave to look into how he could earn a side income.

In 2011, with financial goals in mind, Dave began exploring the idea of starting a business. But instead of building a business to replace his teaching job, he wanted to create a side business online that would provide more financial security and flexibility for his family.

This was a slow part of Dave's story, where he spent nine months researching and learning from other successful business owners. He read over a thousand articles on online business during this time, reading a dozen or so each night after his baby daughter was in bed.

> *That time period of reading was very important. I'm very thankful that I had a paycheck that could provide for my family during that time because I think it was the key to immersing myself in the different ways you can earn income through an online business.*

Early in his research, Dave came across Pat Flynn of *Smart Passive Income*. He probably read everything that Pat had posted on his blog up to that point. It was Pat's "Niche Website Duels" that inspired Dave to think about creating a niche website for a very specific audience.

Dave's first idea was to create an auto body repair website since Crystal's family owned body shops and he found the industry interesting. Although the idea was great, it wasn't a good fit for Dave. Teaching was too time-consuming; he knew he

2011 Starts thinking about creating a side business

Dave Stuart Jr. // 147

didn't have the margin in his life to develop expertise in an unrelated field to teaching. So he focused his blog content on teaching instead.

In one of Pat Flynn's posts, Dave came across Corbett Barr, then of *Think Traffic*. As Corbett, Chase Reeve, and Caleb Wojcik launched their *Fizzle* brand, Dave found himself resonating with their earnest, no-nonsense approach. It was while reading articles by these three that Dave clarified his *why* for starting a blog for teachers: expanding his impact while earning a better income for his family.

> *I figured that impact was the key. It was why I wanted to become a teacher, and it was why I wanted to write since I was a kid. A blog, I started to see, gave me the potential opportunity to encourage and equip teachers, who would then encourage and equip countless students. But beautifully, it would give me a chance to earn extra income for my family at the same time. That was just what I needed.*

With a new perspective and the strong support of his wife, in May of 2012 Dave started blogging under *Teaching the Core*. His plan was to read through a set of controversial teaching standards and parse out what they might look like in his own classroom.

The Turning Point of Dave's Blog

With his second daughter Laura on the way, Dave's family moved into a foreclosed home that needed total remodeling. As a new homeowner, Dave felt the responsibility to provide for his family even more. That summer of 2012, he would grab an energy drink after the kids were in bed, writing his way through a dense but important set of teaching standards, the Common Core.

For the first six months of Dave's blogging journey, he worked at night after everyone was asleep and the day's remodeling work was done. By the close of 2012, he was receiving several dollars a month in Amazon affiliate income from books he recommended on the blog, but Dave knew he needed to create more income.

When thinking back on how the blog survived beyond this point, Dave attributes a lot to Crystal. She believed in the potential of what he was creating, and she took on extra duties around the house to help him see it through. He refers to his wife as "the hero of the story" because, when it became hard to juggle teaching, blogging, and family life, Crystal's toughness, trust, and work ethic made it possible for Dave to persevere.

The first flash of light came about half a year into Dave's blogging journey when he asked his alma mater's marketing department if they would like to advertise on his blog. After sharing his monthly pageviews and presenting his pricing plans

> " A blog . . . gave me the potential opportunity to encourage and equip teachers, who would then encourage and equip countless students.

(a strategy he learned from an old Pat Flynn post), he received a contract: nine months of advertising for $1800.

This advertising collaboration encouraged Dave to look into other opportunities to monetize his blog. In the early spring of 2013, Dave decided to create a Speaking and Workshops page on his website, hoping to attract some speaking gigs to help him gain experience. He linked to the page in blog posts and shared it on his small social media channels. Within a few months, he was hired to speak at events in Oklahoma, Missouri, and his own state of Michigan. To date, Dave has spoken in 25 different states.

> The role that I see my work playing is in encouraging and equipping teachers so that they can promote the long-term flourishing of their students. The encouraging part of that is key.

The role that I see my work playing . . . is in encouraging and equipping teachers so that they can promote the long-term flourishing of their students. The encouraging part of that is key. There are a lot of professional development options out there that equip teachers, but too few of them make the work manageable or motivating. Robust, rigorous encouragement is a key part of what I do.

With an emphasis on encouraging teachers, Dave steadily built a large online audience through his educational blog and email marketing content.

Prioritizing His Blog and Speaking

After publishing consistent blog posts every Tuesday and Saturday for a couple of years, Dave saw his audience slowly and steadily grow. His strategies for audience growth were always kept in check by a simple question: How do *I* like to be treated as a blog reader or an email subscriber?

As his readership steadily grew, Dave saw an increase in speaking engagement requests, emails from readers, and income-generating opportunities.

Though the growth wasn't overnight, within a couple of years Dave was faced with an important decision: How would he handle the success—and the growing demands—of his business?

He knew he didn't want to quit his teaching job, but he also didn't want to keep working nights to make the blog run.

After a period of reflection, Dave decided in 2015 to give up 20% of his teaching salary and teach one less class each day. This meant that his classes would end around 12:00 p.m. every day. That way, he could wrap up his teaching-related duties by 3:00 p.m., giving him a couple of hours each afternoon to do the writing and administrative work of the business.

This change now allows Dave to work on his business early in the morning before his kids wake up and then write from 3:00 to 5:15 p.m. before he goes home for the day. Instead of working into the wee hours of the night, Dave prioritizes family dinners and helping his children with their homework. It also gives him enough time to unwind and spend time with Crystal after a fulfilling day of work. Not overworking has been a critical component of Dave's success since then, as it forces him to do less but better as a blogger and businessman.

It was also during this time that Dave "de-niched" his blog, moving from *Teaching the Core* to *Dave Stuart Jr*. This freed Dave up to write about a broader range of topics for teachers, such as literacy, motivation, and the inner work of teaching.

2015 Cuts back on teaching hours to spend more time on the business

How Dave Balances Work and Life

In addition to his day job, Dave continues to lead workshops and speak at conferences around the nation. Up until 2018, speaking engagements accounted for the majority of his business income at 65%, while his second largest income stream came from digital products. This meant too much time away from family, however, so in 2018 Dave worked to transition the business into a product-centric model.

For years, Dave has offered a handful of starter kits on his website with a "pay what you want" model, which has been successful since Dave's readers have been generous with what they feel the starter kits are worth. In addition to these, he publishes several eBooks for colleagues he has met with strong offerings for his readers, as well as an eBook of his own.

But the turning point for Dave's product income stream has come from developing online courses for teachers. In 2016, he built a course called Teaching with Articles, and in 2018 he launched his flagship course called Student Motivation Course.

In a single month, this course brought in more revenue than Dave does in a year as a teacher. The training model Dave is experimenting with is finding rave reviews with his first cohorts of participants.

In 2014, Dave's work on the niche he started in culminated in a traditionally published a book titled *A Non-Freaked Out Guide to Teaching the Common Core*. It was a surreal moment to see his words in print for the first time, a dream he's had for as long as he can remember. The Common Core, however, was never a strong passion of Dave's, which has made him eager to publish a more timeless book.

With the July 2018 release of *These Six Things: How to Focus Your Teaching on What Matters Most*, Dave is happy to have written a book he can proudly recommend. Even with these books published, Dave still considers blogging to be his medium of choice.

> *Being a blogger, to me, means being a writer. I love being a blogger because, unlike the writers of old, you can get stuff out the door really fast. It's way better than getting an article in some prestigious journal or writing a book because with blogging . . . I get feedback today. Did today's post help someone? That's what being a blogger is really about.*

In the next few years, Dave will continue to blog and teach simultaneously. He hopes to build more online courses and digital products, as he has lots of ideas but limited time. He's also thrilled to earn triple the income of his current teaching position through his online business and gets excited at the prospect of giving a growing percentage of that income to causes he and his wife believe in.

With more financial security and a more flexible schedule, Dave can prioritize his greatest earthly treasure: his family. As a husband and father of four children,

he's thankful for the support of his wife, the school he works for, and his blog's readership of colleagues around the world.

> *The kids just balance out my life. I go home, and I'm immediately yanked into their world: playing, wrestling, chasing them around, getting mobbed by them . . . While I love the teachers and students that my work serves, these kids are why I put in the extra hours, put myself out there, and hustle. So you can't tell the story of my business without the story of my family. It's not possible.*

Although Dave's days of living paycheck to paycheck seem like a long time ago, he still remembers those first few years teaching in Michigan with humility and gratitude. Because of his consistent application of the principles he learned during those months of reading about blogging—and because of his wife's consistent willingness to take on a bigger workload to make it all work—their family's finances are now supported by his blog. The many blessings they experience are possible because of a website that, once upon a time in May 2012, had never had a visitor. And, Dave is quick to add, all kinds of providence, too.

From finally getting that rug for their living room to taking his family on trips, Dave has found joy in providing for his family through both writing and teaching—all while continuing to do what he loves.

Now when Dave takes the stage during a speaking gig, he proudly stands in front of an audience of fellow educators and introduces himself as a teacher and a blogger.

The Business Today

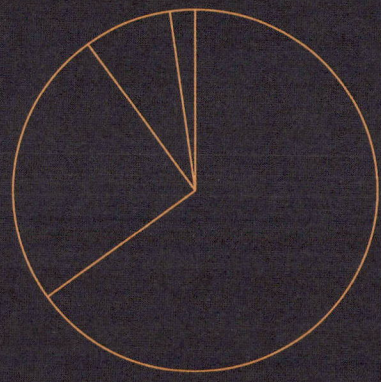

Revenue Breakdown

65% Digital products

25% Speaking/workshops

8% Traditional publishing

2% Affiliate sales

By the Numbers

35,000 Blog readers per month

15,000 Email subscribers

Products & Services

- Pop-Up Debate Starter Kit
- School Year Starter Kit
- Student Motivation Course
- Teaching with Articles course
- *Mechanics Instruction that Sticks* eBook series
- *The Write Structure* and *Never Finished: Continually Becoming the Teachers We Want to Be* eBooks
- *A Non-Freaked Out Guide to Teaching the Common Core* and *These 6 Things: How to Focus Your Teaching on What Matters Most* traditional books

Revenue Growth

2013 — $5,000

2017 — $125,000

davestuartjr.com

Sarah Morgan

Online Business Owner. Circus Performer. Teacher. Blogger.

WORDS BY KAYLA HOLLATZ • PHOTOGRAPHY BY CALEB WOJCIK

Sitting on her front porch, seven year old Sarah Morgan zipped up her puffy coat and put its hood over her head. Braving the early Michigan winter chill, she settled in for a day of selling cookies.

Instead of creating a full-blown recipe with secret ingredients, Sarah took a more simple approach. She threw some chocolate chips and pre-made batter into a bowl and called it good. She was more excited about selling the cookies anyway.

Pulling out a piece of cardboard and a permanent marker, she created a For Sale sign for her cookies. Despite her hard work, foot traffic around her childhood home was lower than usual because of the crisp November air, so she didn't sell any. This only motivated her to try selling more things as she grew up.

> I told myself, "I'm going to make this thing and people will buy it." Nobody actually bought anything, but I just liked making stuff.

Sarah has always been a self-starter. As a teenager, she learned how to code by digging through other people's websites in the early days of AOL internet. She found a site that was purple and featured a one-column layout, so Sarah copied the code to achieve a similar look. Her first website was on gurlPages with her name colorfully displayed in the top banner.

While she regrets not adding more white space to her early designs, she wasn't afraid to tweak her code until she got it just right. Instead of taking classes or reading books on web design, she jumped right in and figured it out by trial and error.

> *Nobody else has the crazy idea that if they want to make something, they can just go ahead and make it. They're waiting for permission from someone to tell them they can ... but I don't care about getting anybody's permission.*

1997 Creates her first website

Deciding on a Career Path

As she approached college, Sarah was more focused on what she didn't want to do than what she did want to pursue. Since she wanted to avoid all math courses, she decided to pursue a degree in journalism. She was soon hired at a television station in Detroit.

Even though Sarah had a writing position at the station, her team knew she had design skills too.

As the internet and social media platforms became more important in news reporting, the station transitioned Sarah into working on design full-time.

Initially, her desk was tucked in a corner away from the newsroom. It provided a nice, quiet space for her to focus on writing assignments without the commotion of reporters around her. As an introvert, she loved being in a small shared space with only three other people.

But when the newsroom was fully renovated, Sarah had to move to the center of the newsroom. Now she was surrounded by dozens of noisy reporters and was constantly interrupted by the latest breaking news story. As her working environment changed, she became less interested in her work at the station.

> *I was panicking because I thought I didn't like design anymore. I didn't like coming to work, and I didn't know what else I would do. I didn't want to be a journalist, and I didn't have any other skills or passions.*

Not knowing how to pivot her career, she started freelancing for other clients in her last year at the television station, picking up odd website design gigs for around one hundred dollars each. Through freelancing, Sarah quickly learned she still wanted to pursue design; she just didn't want to do it at the television station any longer.

2011 Starts freelancing

Becoming a Circus Performer

Around this time in 2010, Sarah discovered aerial arts. After going through a difficult breakup, she and a friend bought tickets to an eight-week series of aerial classes. Sarah laughs when she remembers how bad they both were in the first few months. She didn't have the muscle or flexibility to do much of anything. But despite its challenges, she kept going back.

After performing in a student showcase, she partnered with a friend to do a trapeze act at an erotic art festival in 2011. Her first paid gig was a total hit, and she continued to book shows around the Detroit area. Her favorite performance was during a Halloween party where she was hired with friends to do a bearded lady routine. The crowd absolutely loved it.

The more shows she did, the more she considered teaching aerial arts. After teaching for two years in smaller spaces, she stumbled upon the perfect opportunity when she met a music teacher who had recently bought a studio space with twenty-foot ceilings.

The music teacher wanted circus performers to teach students and generate enough money to pay for the rest of the space. Sarah started working for the music teacher and learned a lot about running a small business while also getting to focus on what she loved most: teaching and performing.

2010 Discovers aerial arts

2013 Starts teaching aerial arts

> Nobody else has the crazy idea that if they want to make something, they can just go ahead and make it. They're waiting for permission for someone to tell them they can… but I don't care about getting anybody's permission.

Quitting Her Full-Time Job

After seven years at the television station, Sarah knew it was time to get serious about her plans to quit her day job. Circus performing and freelancing were going well, and both income streams were giving her more fulfillment than her job.

In 2011, she made a goal in September to leave her position after one more year. This would give her enough time to create a solid client base and book enough aerial shows to grow her income.

Nine months later, Sarah was spending more time freelancing at her desk than working on her work assignments. During her performance review, her boss said he could tell that she wasn't passionate about her work anymore and they needed to find a solution.

> *I remember going back to my desk and thinking, "Holy shit. I have to leave my job in a month. This is it. They're forcing me into doing this." I grabbed my notepad . . . and wrote: I need to buy a laptop, I need to figure out health insurance, and I need to figure out all of this stuff.*

She promptly quit her job a month later in 2012—and instead of giving a two weeks' notice, she told her boss her last day would be the following day because of how many circus shows she had booked. The first thing she did was buy six gourmet cupcakes to celebrate her big leap into the unknown world of freelancing and blogging. She didn't know what to expect but she knew anything would be better than the nine to five routine.

Full-Time Blogging

Sarah's initial plan was to freelance while continuing to grow her blog audience and book aerial gigs on the side, giving her multiple streams of income. She also decided to merge her personal blog with her design portfolio under the name *XOSarah*. Sarah spent most of her days happily writing and designing on her laptop from the comfort of her couch.

After two years of full-time blogging and freelancing, she moved from Detroit to San Diego in 2014 for a change of scenery. Even though she downsized from a house to a small apartment, she was happier than ever before.

> " I remember just sitting in my kitchen and thinking, "Oh my god. I make more money blogging than I did at my corporate job. I'm here. I made it."

> *I remember just sitting in my kitchen and thinking, "Oh my god. I make more money blogging than I did at my corporate job. I'm here. I made it."*

As *XOSarah* grew, she added Amazon affiliate links to her blog posts and started doing influencer affiliate partnerships with some of the tools she uses to run her blog. She also wrote an eBook and took on a couple of consulting gigs each month for a few years.

Focusing on passive income, she also built online courses that would help other bloggers grow their online presence with tips she learned after twenty years of blogging. With more than five streams of income, Sarah was able to transition out of freelance web design into full-time blogging and teaching in 2016.

Sarah's Business Today

As an online educator, Sarah runs multiple courses with live coaching calls and community support in addition to creating free weekly content. She also has a membership community, *Dare to Grow*, that keeps her in the thick of her industry mentoring bloggers and small business owners.

Sarah still enjoys spending most of her days writing and designing from her couch. While her life may not look glamorous from the outside, she has found a rhythm that really works for her.

> *I usually hang out with my dog and work on the internet. I teach aerial two days a week and train two or three days. I will totally put away my work and go to the beach or go hiking. I try to take advantage of my flexible schedule.*

After experimenting with all kinds of digital products, Sarah can now laser focus on the best fitting offerings for her fast-growing blog audience and chill lifestyle.

With two decades of blogging and design experience fueling her work, Sarah never runs out of advice to share. But she isn't just creating content to add to the noise. One of her email subscribers says that Sarah's emails are always the "cheerful kick in the ass" she needs to start her week.

It's that tough love approach and her "no permission necessary" attitude that mark Sarah as a true influencer in her field.

The Business Today

Revenue Breakdown

70% Courses   **20%** eBooks   **10%** Affiliate sales

Product Success

$1,100 Sales from first eBook (2013)   **$3,500** Sales from first course (2014)

By the Numbers

60,000 Website views per month

20,000 Email subscribers

$27,000 Revenue generated in the first year of *XOSarah*

Products & Services

- *Dare to Grow* membership site
- Dare to Email course
- The Productive Solopreneur course
- Pinterest Powerhouse course
- Content & blog planning workbooks
- eBooks
- Website reviews

xosarah.com

Tyler James

Comic Creator. Graphic Novelist. Podcaster. Blogger.

WORDS BY KAYLA HOLLATZ • PHOTOGRAPHY BY MAUREEN COTTON

Nestled under the twinkling lights of his family's Christmas tree was a large gift-wrapped present with Tyler James' name on it. His mind went wild as he tried to guess what was inside it each day leading up to Christmas.

To his surprise and delight, on Christmas Day Tyler found a professional drawing table hidden underneath the snowman-covered wrapping paper. It came with an adjustable lamp that was perfect for creating art into the wee hours of the night with his childhood friend Matt. Of the two, Tyler was the better storyteller. He went on to sell his first hand-drawn comic book at just fourteen years old in 1993.

That was around the same time that Image Comics was founded. Before digital comics were available, it felt impossible to read the full storyline of popular superheroes like Batman and Spiderman because many of the first issues were rare and too expensive for teens.

> **"** It was definitely a cool feeling that kids were asking when the next issue was coming out.

Image Comics created a whole new superhero universe that allowed readers like Tyler to experience the hero's story from the very first issue. This kind of accessibility gave Tyler a whole new appreciation and passion for comics.

Tyler would eventually go from a kid selling comics out of his backpack to creating a six-figure comics blog and publishing business. But before he launched his blog, he spent years collecting skills that would later help him become an innovative entrepreneur.

Discovering His Passion for Comics

The first thing that inspired Tyler to step into a local comic book shop in his hometown of Albany, New York, was the bleeding Superman logo on the front cover of the *Death of Superman* issue.

1993 Sold his first hand-drawn comic book

From then on, he became a regular at the comic book shop. Since many of the employees and regulars were older with edgy tattoos and piercings, Tyler felt cool just walking through the aisles of comics.

Each week, he would thumb through comic books and plan when he could purchase each one. He used much of his weekly allowance to pay for newer issues he could afford. But it wasn't enough just to read comic books. Tyler also wanted to create his own superheroes.

After two years of creating comics for himself, Tyler decided to sell double-sided copies of his own comics. The first comic book he sold was about an unstoppable assassin with luck powers called Upset.

As a teenager, he sold a total of nine copies at one dollar apiece—with most of them being purchased by friends at school and one by his supportive uncle, who insisted on getting an autographed copy.

> *I think the first issue was about ten pages. It was definitely a cool feeling that kids were asking when the next issue was coming out.*

Tyler kept drawing comics in his spare time until college where he dropped the art form almost completely.

Reshifting His Priorities

Tyler went to Washington, D.C., to attend Georgetown University right after graduating high school. Being somewhat of a jack-of-all-trades, he had a hard time choosing a specific career path to pursue—and creating comics was an afterthought.

As he inched closer to graduation, Tyler felt a call to give back. Teach For America seemed like a great program to get involved with, and it would buy him two more years to figure out what he wanted to do next. With that, he accepted a teaching position in New Orleans.

> *I quickly found that there was going to be no time for creative work. It literally sucked every ounce of energy from me. After teaching for a full day and then doing some grading, I only had enough time to watch Jack Bauer save the world on 24 and he saved me in those two years too.*

Teach For America challenged Tyler and left him exhausted, so once his two-year commitment was up, he moved back to Washington, D.C. He soon found an opportunity to work with the American Institutes of Research in 2003, which provided him with much-needed stability after his Teach For America experience.

While there, Tyler stumbled upon a continuing education class on comic book script writing. Feeling incredibly out of practice and inspired to reignite his creativity, Tyler signed up. After being a self-taught artist for so many years, Tyler was excited to learn from an expert in the field.

> ❝ **After teaching for a full day and then doing some grading, I only had enough time to watch Jack Bauer save the world on *24* and he saved me in those two years too.**

> *I took the class, and it sort of got the ball rolling again creatively.*
>
> *It got me to start drawing and writing again. In that class, I wrote what would become the first book I would actually take, get printed, and sell again.*

The Beginning of a New Side Hustle

In his mid-twenties, Tyler still didn't consider comics to be a viable career path, but his desire to connect with other comic creators led him to create *ComixTribe*. The original mission statement for the group is—and will continue to be—"Creators helping creators make better comics."

Before co-founding *ComixTribe* with editor Steven Forbes, the duo worked together on one of Tyler's comic books. The first time Tyler received Steven's script edits, he couldn't believe how many red marks he saw. Tyler remembers it looking like a murder scene, but he really valued Steven's point of view. It was their first of many collaborations.

Around that time in 2011, Tyler and Steven found their best source of revenue came from selling comic books at comic conventions. This taught them a lot about what it took to properly package, print, market, and sell comics.

> *One of the challenges is that the profit margins on comics are abysmal. It's very tough, especially when you're talking about indie comics. It's tough not to lose money because it's such a labor-intensive thing.*

Then a new player came into the mix: Kickstarter crowdfunding. Tyler decided to experiment with a Kickstarter campaign in 2012 just to see what would happen. He set a goal for $8,500 but ended up raising $26,000. That was more revenue than *ComixTribe* had made in the last two years.

> *What ended up happening with the success from that Kickstarter... was that more of my time was being pulled away from the* ComixTribe *site and put into building the publishing line.*

Tyler originally thought the Kickstarter campaign would be a one-time project but he wanted to see if he could replicate the success of the first comic. Never shying away from a challenge, he launched a children's book through *ComixTribe* called *C is for Cthulhu* in 2014 that went on to generate $120,000 in sales, far more than he had ever anticipated.

2011 Started *ComixTribe*

2012 Launched a Kickstarter campaign

> "I've never been more excited to go to work every day.

A new Kickstarter-Inspired Business

With *ComixTribe*'s success on Kickstarter, Tyler began to see an untapped opportunity to inspire and educate other creators on how to have the same success for their own projects.

Embracing this new niche led him to create the *ComixLaunch* brand in 2015. Knowing that only 49% of comic-creator Kickstarters were being fully funded at the time, Tyler set out to improve that percentage by providing creators with exclusive resources, courses, and consulting. The success rate of comics on Kickstarter has now raised to 54% over the past three years, even as the average Kickstarter success rate has dropped.

Tyler wanted to reach as many content creators as possible so he also created a podcast that focuses on providing tips and tricks for creators who want to learn how to fully fund their Kickstarter. He's excited to continue working on the membership community he started for *ComixLaunch* as well as interviewing creators who inspire him on his podcast.

ComixTribe is also alive and well. The website still hosts some of the most read how-to content for comic creators on the internet. Their latest crime-horror series,

SINK, has set new company sales records and is in talks for adaptation to film and television.

After building several brands from the ground up, Tyler decided to pursue his passion for comics and Kickstarter marketing as a full-time creator in 2017.

> *I've never been more excited to go to work every day. It's still hard sometimes on a day-to-day basis when you feel like you're sort of walking without a safety net underneath you. But then I see the creators that I've worked with have now raised over $325,000 in funding for their own dream projects . . . That's fun.*

Quitting his day job wasn't an easy decision, but after one year of full-time entrepreneurship under his belt, Tyler is still energized by his work. He usually starts his day at 6 a.m. with meditation and a slow-paced breakfast before transitioning into answering emails and setting his "Big 3" goals for the day.

When he's ready to unwind from work, he has a signature shut-down routine that helps him process through all of his daily completed tasks while jotting down three things he's thankful for. Quality time with his family always makes it onto his gratitude list.

> *Since I get to make my own hours and the value I create isn't tied directly to hours clocked in, I'm currently able to make every Thursday a "daddy day" off of work to take care of my newborn son, Cullen. My wife, step-daughter, and I are absolutely smitten with the little guy.*

Working from the same professional drawing table he received as a kid, Tyler draws comics with an unmistakable passion for the craft. As he adjusts the lamp hovering above his comic panels, he finds peace in returning to the art form that started it all.

The Business Today

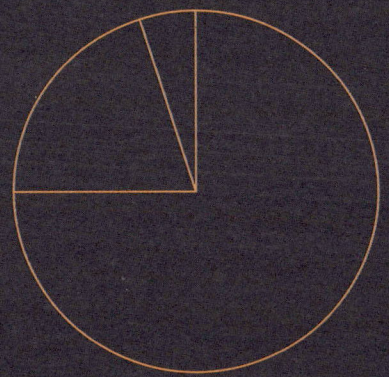

Revenue Breakdown

75% Books & merchandise

20% Courses & memberships

5% Affiliate sales & sponsorships

By the Numbers

4,000 Blog readers per month

31,000 Email subscribers

$2,800 Earned from 8 students in the pilot version of The ComixLaunch Course

Products & Services

- *ComixLaunch Pro* membership and courses
- *ComixLaunch MasterMind*
- *ComixTribe* comics and graphic novels
- *C is for Cthulhu* children's books and toys

Kickstarter Launches

2012 *OXYMORON* Hardcover Graphic Novel
GOAL **$8,000** → RAISED **$26,000**

2017 *Sweet Dreams Cthulhu*
GOAL **$15,000** → RAISED **$105,827**

comixtribe.com

Mique Provost

Wife. Special Needs Mom. Creative Entrepreneur. Blogger.

WORDS BY KAYLA HOLLATZ • PHOTOGRAPHY BY CALEB WOJCIK

Even with her unmistakable entrepreneurial spirit, Mique Provost always knew she wanted to be a wife and mom above all else.

> *The goal was always to stay at home with my family. When people would say, "What do you want do?", I would say, "Be a wife and a mom."*

But while her heart was always set on starting a family, Mique still wasn't willing to give up on her other aspirations. One day she would combine her passion for motherhood and entrepreneurship through her blog *Thirty Handmade Days*, but she had other business ideas to test out beforehand.

As a teen, instead of running a typical babysitting business, she differentiated herself by creating business cards, giving progress reports to the child's parents, and even throwing a few parties for the kids. She had a knack for taking things one step further than all the other teenage babysitters on the block.

And even though she grew up in the laid-back culture of Encinitas, California, her parents always encouraged Mique's entrepreneurial dreams, especially her dad who was an entrepreneur himself.

> *Both my parents made me feel like I could do whatever I wanted if I put my mind to it and worked hard enough.*

Taking after her parents, Mique pursued small business ventures until high school graduation. Then she enrolled in college in Utah for a few semesters before she made the tough decision not to finish her college degree when the chance to be a wife and mom appeared.

Becoming a Full-Time Mom

Mique met her husband Josh in Utah while she was in college. They met through their roommates that were dating the day Josh moved from LA. Josh and Mique had their first date in January when she was twenty years old and he was twenty-two. After spending every second outside of class together, they were married in August of that same year.

Shortly after exchanging their vows, Josh's parents asked him to run the family business—a collection agency in California. Though this wasn't Josh's dream job, he was a hard worker and good at it. After talking it over, they both decided it was the right move.

But right before they moved from Utah to Burbank, Mique found out she was pregnant with twins. Sadly, just two days before their move, Mique lost the babies due to a miscarriage.

With so much change and chaos happening all at once, she had a difficult time grieving during her

big life transition. But shortly after moving to Burbank, Mique discovered she was pregnant again.

> *I was scared because I had already experienced the miscarriage the first time. . . and I didn't want to go through that again.*

The anxiety she had around her second pregnancy was alleviated by the great community she built in Burbank, which prepared Mique to give birth to a sweet, happy, and hyper little boy named Jonathan in 2000. Finally, she could settle into her new life as a stay-at-home mom.

A Life-Changing Diagnosis

When Jonathan was two years old, Mique's father-in-law mentioned that Jonathan wasn't answering when his name was called. He didn't know how to talk yet either. Noticing that his development wasn't progressing, Mique started researching and learning more about autism.

2000 Gives birth to Jonathan

After reading a list of autism traits and characteristics, Mique found that Jonathan fit all of them. This revelation came near the end of her next pregnancy—their daughter Julia was born in 2002.

When they received the official diagnosis from a doctor in 2003, Josh and Mique immediately sprang into action. They had different ideas on how to care for Jonathan, but they both agreed that therapy would provide a healthy place to start.

Mique thought that if they started therapy early, Jonathan might make huge improvements by the time he was six or seven. While he made some progress, it was clear that he had a more severe level of autism.

Launching a Family Blog

As their family faced challenges head-on, Mique gave birth to her third child, Drew, in 2006. A year later, her sister remembered that Mique always enjoyed writing and thought it could be a good creative outlet. This inspired Mique to create a blog.

> *I've always tried to have an outlet. I took a hip-hop class and a photography class. I just needed a little bit of time away from being a wife and mom. This blog was my outlet. In the beginning, it was all about connecting with other people and sharing ideas. I had no idea . . . that it could turn into a business.*

At first, Mique focused on creating a personal blog where she published family photos and shared stories of their everyday life in California. While she loved sharing an inside look into her family life through the blog, she wanted to turn it into more of a resource center for creative projects.

2002 Daughter Julia is born

2003 Jonathan is diagnosed with autism

> **This blog was my outlet. In the beginning, it was all about connecting with other people and sharing ideas. I had no idea that it could turn into a business.**

> **Earning money felt exciting because I went from nothing to earning something. I had been blogging for so long at that point. It was validating.**

With this change, she found that her project-inspired roundup posts started to really take off. Once she saw the content taking over her family blog, she decided to launch a separate blog under the name *Thirty Handmade Days* in 2008.

For the next few years, Mique spent most of her time hosting giveaways on her website and crafting roundup blog posts of projects other people were creating. This was all done in between taking care of her kids.

In 2011, Mique was inspired to post more original content on *Thirty Handmade Days*. After more than four years of blogging about other people's projects, she decided to share her own recipes, design advice, and other things she was working on.

It also helped that Drew was off to kindergarten and both Jonathan and Julia were in school full-time. Since Mique had more time to devote to her creative outlet, she took her blog more seriously than ever before.

At first Josh didn't understand why she spent so much time on the blog, but she kept growing her audience and making connections with other bloggers.

Then a few of her blogging friends suggested Mique put ads on her website through Google AdSense in 2011. These ads created the first blog income for Mique bringing in $6.25 each month in the beginning.

> *Earning money felt exciting because I went from nothing to earning something. I had been blogging for so long at that point. It was validating, like I'm not just putting stuff out there and people are only commenting. That's validating on its own, but earning income is a different kind of validation.*

Introducing Multiple Streams of Income

For the next two years, Mique attended blogger conferences and spent much of her spare time learning about business. She loved researching, reading, and experimenting with new skills, so it was an exciting time for her.

She also introduced sponsored content around this time as her website traffic and Twitter following grew. Pinterest had just launched and was quickly becoming a game changer for bloggers who wanted to drive more traffic to their website.

2008 Launches *Thirty Handmade Days*

2011 Earns her first dollar from her blog

> There's always going to be somebody who has it better than you and someone who has it worse. You just need to be okay with who you are, where you are.

Wanting to introduce an extra stream of income, she decided to offer printable digital products on her website in late 2015. Rather than niche down to a specific topic, she wanted to share resources for moms to simplify their lives through organization, cleaning, parenting, cooking, and more.

These printables have continually been a top performing—and somewhat surprising—source of income for her family. With ads, sponsorships, digital products, and affiliate income, Mique saw that her blog was generating substantial revenue.

With her blog quickly turning into a full-time job, Mique embraced entrepreneurship. Her dad was so proud of everything she had created. But at the height of her blog's success, she found out her dad had cancer, and in the same year, lost him.

Mique's dad had always been her strongest supporter and loudest cheerleader. So much of what she learned about entrepreneurship and parenting came from watching him do both with grace and love.

> *My dad hasn't been able to see all these exciting blogging opportunities and things that I'm doing now. I know it sounds so cheesy, but I still feel like he can see it all happening. But I would love to be able to call him and say, "Hey, Dad, look."*

Losing her dad caused Mique to reestablish her priorities and spend more time with her family than ever. Her husband's faith in the blog began to grow, and she kept adding to her family's income through the blog while continuing to take care of her kids.

An Important Decision

In 2015, Jonathan hit puberty and Mique faced a whole new set of obstacles.

Even after different types of therapy and some time on medication, Mique started to notice that Jonathan wasn't getting better. When Jonathan became more physically aggressive toward Mique, she knew a bigger conversation with Josh needed to happen.

It took months for Mique and Josh to wrestle with the idea of Jonathan living in a group home full-time. But after visiting a group home in the area, they instantly knew it would be the right place for Jonathan. It was a difficult decision for them, but they knew it was in the best interest of Jonathan and their family.

> *I try to imagine it being like Jonathan is in college early, because that's what it feels like. He comes home once a month now, and we try to do fun things and the stuff he loves to do. He seems happy. He's doing really well, and he's progressing.*

As her family settled into their new routine, she began sharing her story on the blog. It helped her connect with like-minded readers who offered empathetic words of encouragement—and her business continued to grow.

Mique's Business Today

What started as a hobby blog has turned into a five person team operation ten years later. Advertising, brand sponsorships, digital products, and affiliate income still make up the majority of Mique's income today. But instead of creating all of the content on her own, she has a team of contributors to help.

In 2016, she also added Josh to her growing team. It took Mique a full year to convince Josh to leave his full-time position to help her with the blog. He finally put in his two weeks' notice after he discovered that the company he worked for wouldn't give him the opportunity to work from home in the future.

> My dad hasn't been able to see all these exciting blogging opportunities and things that I'm doing now. I know it sounds so cheesy, but I still feel like he can see it all happening.

As a natural-born entrepreneur, she has a hard time turning off and unwinding at the end of the day. While she loves what she does for a living, she also realizes how important it is to cherish the time she has with her husband and three kids in every season of life.

Like many bloggers, Mique has also struggled with comparison, but she often remembers wise words that her father would say when doubt starts to creep in:

> *There's always going to be somebody who has it better than you and someone who has it worse. You just need to be okay with who you are, where you are.*

She leads her business team with the same authenticity and vulnerability as she does with her family, perfectly blending her two worlds together.

■

The Business Today

Revenue Breakdown

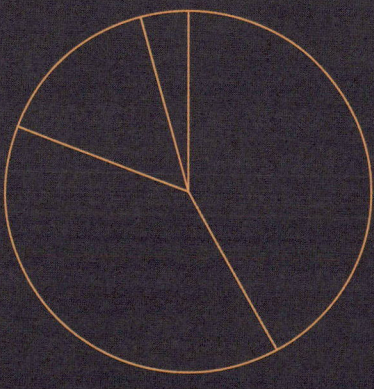

42% Sponsorships
39% Ads
15% Affiliate sales
4% Digital products

By the Numbers

 1,500,000
Blog readers per month

 45,000
Email subscribers

Products & Services

- Budget and planning binders
- *Delicious Dinners in Under An Hour* eBook
- Quote printables
- *Make & Share Random Acts of Kindness* book

Average Monthly Income

2008 — $0 — Created blog
2011 — $6.25 — Started using AdSense
2015 — $30,000 — Added digital products

thirtyhandmadedays.com

The Fantasy Footballers

Podcasters. Sports Fans. Marketers. Entertainers. Bloggers.

WORDS BY KAYLA HOLLATZ • PHOTOGRAPHY BY CALEB WOJCIK

pon entering *The Fantasy Footballers* studio space, it's impossible to miss the passion Jason Moore, Andy Holloway, and Mike Wright have for football.

Their podcast studio walls are lined with football trading cards, framed football jerseys, and sports newspaper clippings. Dozens of iconic player figurines are displayed on a desk next to a gift from a listener—a pair of Vans shoes painted with their podcast logo.

After getting a tour of the space, it's safe to assume this trio lives and breathes football, and you'd be correct. But turning their favorite hobby into a thriving business wasn't on their radar—until they invited others to join the conversations they were already having inside their fantasy football league.

Early Career Dreams

Andy and Jason met each other in a fantasy basketball league in high school. Jason invited Andy to join the league, and they have been hooked on fantasy sports ever since.

Mike was a part of a few fantasy basketball, baseball, and football leagues in his early twenties. He jokes about how he missed his first fantasy football league's draft so he had to do an autodraft. He did terrible that year, but he learned his lesson and hasn't missed a draft since. Luckily, Mike has won a few championships since then to redeem himself.

While Mike, Jason, and Andy all loved fantasy sports growing up, they had very different career aspirations. In high school, Andy and Jason began working together on Jason's first business operation in 1999, Nothin' But Net Web Design. Jason was in charge of sales and paid Andy pennies for the design.

While Jason and Andy felt like natural-born entrepreneurs, Mike was more interested in music. He had a knack for audio editing and performing, so he wanted to be a rock star or a professional studio musician. He saw himself as a freelancer but never had aspirations of becoming the boss.

However, Mike did have a business idea in grade school to rent out some of his best Nintendo games to other kids at recess. Modeling Blockbuster's rental service, he started making a small profit from his video game collection. This passion for gaming led Mike to join a video game company where he met Andy and Jason in 2010.

1999 Andy and Jason work together on Nothin' But Net Web Design

Working Together at a Video Game Company

For eight years, Andy worked as a web developer at a game studio that was run by Jason. Mike joined the company later as their audio guy.

While working together, they learned a lot about how to use social media, marketing, and SEO to build a company. They each had a different set of skills and quickly found their ideal workflow.

To survive their hour long commute to work, Andy and Mike constantly listened to fantasy football podcasts. The more they listened to podcasts, the more they had to talk about over lunch. They loved heckling each other and trash-talking in the breakroom.

2010 Mike meets Andy and Jason

During the 2014 football season, Mike and Andy decided to start a private podcast for their ten other leaguemates. Inside these episodes, the friendly banter was in no short supply. They were completely free to be themselves and "destroy each other," as Jason puts it.

After hearing that their leaguemates loved the podcast, Mike and Andy decided to publish the episodes publicly. But once it went live and the podcast felt more real, Jason could tell that Mike and Andy were more buttoned-up in their conversations. They weren't taking the same playful jabs at each other like they were when it was private. Mike admits now that he felt like they were acting, and it put them in a box.

> *When you are consuming tons of other content or you're an entrepreneur, you've got to find your own voice and find whatever special or unique thing you have to say.* —Andy

Seeing the need for improvement and direction, they decided to take a step back and reassess what they wanted the podcast to be. It felt like the market for fantasy football resources was already saturated, so they spent time defining what they wanted *The Fantasy Footballers* to uniquely provide its listeners.

Jason wasn't originally a part of the podcast, but when he told Mike and Andy about all the potential he saw in it, they decided to have him join in in 2015. Jason had great business experience and their mix of personalities was perfect for the show.

After joining *The Fantasy Footballers*, Jason was in the middle of his own business transition. His video game company was about to go under, and he didn't have a solid plan B.

As a husband and father of three who wanted to provide for his family, Jason got a temporary part-time job at T-Mobile selling phones while selling real estate and hosting the podcast show on the side. He was determined to make the business a sustainable source of income for his family.

> **When you are consuming tons of other content or you're an entrepreneur, you've got to find your own voice and find whatever special or unique thing you have to say.**

During this transition time, the guys were starting to notice how quickly the podcast was growing. Their podcast download stats were increasing exponentially each week, and more sponsorship opportunities were coming their way. It got to the point where *The Fantasy Footballers* couldn't keep their pace of growth with a part-time effort.

Mike, Andy, and Jason all had conversations with their wives about the potential of quitting their jobs in order to pursue the podcast full-time. They also set goals for what the podcast could grow into and made sure their values were all aligned.

> *We sat down, the three of us, once we took this leap and said, "What do we want this podcast to be?" We didn't have blind aspirations of "Let's just see what happens." We wanted something secure that allows us to have good family lives. Something where we can spend time with our wives and our children, knowing our bills are covered. —Jason*

With this intention in mind, they all quit their day jobs to focus solely on building *The Fantasy Footballers* brand in 2015. From the outside, it may have looked like they were trying to make money by simply watching football and talking about it, but their first year of business solidified how much work actually needed to be done.

2015 Jason joins the podcast

2015 All quit their day jobs

Full-Time Effort Into the Podcast

In their first year, Mike, Andy, and Jason were all working out of Andy's house in a spare bedroom that acted as their recording studio. Mike's wife would take care of the kids downstairs and try to make sure they didn't come into the room when the trio was recording an episode.

Jason's first office space was in a closet in the spare bedroom lovingly referred to as the "cloffice." Working out of Mike's home didn't give them the kind of work-life balance they were hoping for, but they had their eyes on the bigger prize.

In the beginning, they were just trying to get a big enough advertising deal every month so they could keep the podcast going. It caused them to take a few bad deals, but they learned a lot through the process and now walk into term negotiations with more confidence.

The biggest challenge in their first year was working out the kinks of running a seasonal business. Because the regular NFL season is from September to December—not including the draft, preseason, and postseason games—they needed to create strong income streams for off-season months.

Knowing that they had more flextime in the off-season, they decided to create a digital product that listeners would love. After thinking about what they would want as fantasy league fans themselves, they created the Ultimate Draft Kit in the fall of 2016. This digital product helps their listeners plan and choose their top draft selections before the draft so they are always a few steps ahead of other leaguemates.

> *Thankfully, by process of elimination... we landed on an idea that pushed us beyond our expectations and took away the month-to-month worries. Only in this last podcast season have we talked about how nice it is that we don't have to take bad deals. It's really not the freedom of, "Oh, good, we're not going to go under." It's, "We can operate how we want to now."*
> —Jason

As the draft kit sales started to climb, they explored other income streams outside of advertising and brand sponsorships. Since they run an independent podcast show, they thought Patreon would be a perfect fit. Fans of *The Fantasy Footballers* show, who are called the "Foot Clan," can support the podcast by pledging a desired amount each month through Patreon and in return, they receive rewards and exclusive access to episodes.

Of all the success *The Fantasy Footballers* team has had in the last two years, they are most proud of their strong patron and listener support.

> *One of the things we said in the very beginning is every new listener matters. They aren't just this big clump of numbers. I respond to as many people as possible. You took time out of your day to ask me a question; I'll try to answer it.* —Mike

In the past two years, they have intentionally crafted a show that provides a fun, relaxing environment for all fantasy football fanatics. While fantasy football centers around competition, the trio takes a more playful approach with their family-friendly show.

2017 Move into new studio

Their Business Today

After moving into their new studio in January of 2017, they now have ample space for recording podcast episodes, watching football games all day Sunday with their families, and hosting ping pong matches between meetings. This day-to-day rhythm is working considering they received over thirty million podcast downloads during their 2017 podcast season.

Even with their expansive growth during the last two years, they've always kept family as their number one priority. They also attribute much of their success to their wives.

> ❝ One of the things we said in the very beginning is every new listener matters. They aren't just this big clump of numbers. I respond to as many people as possible.

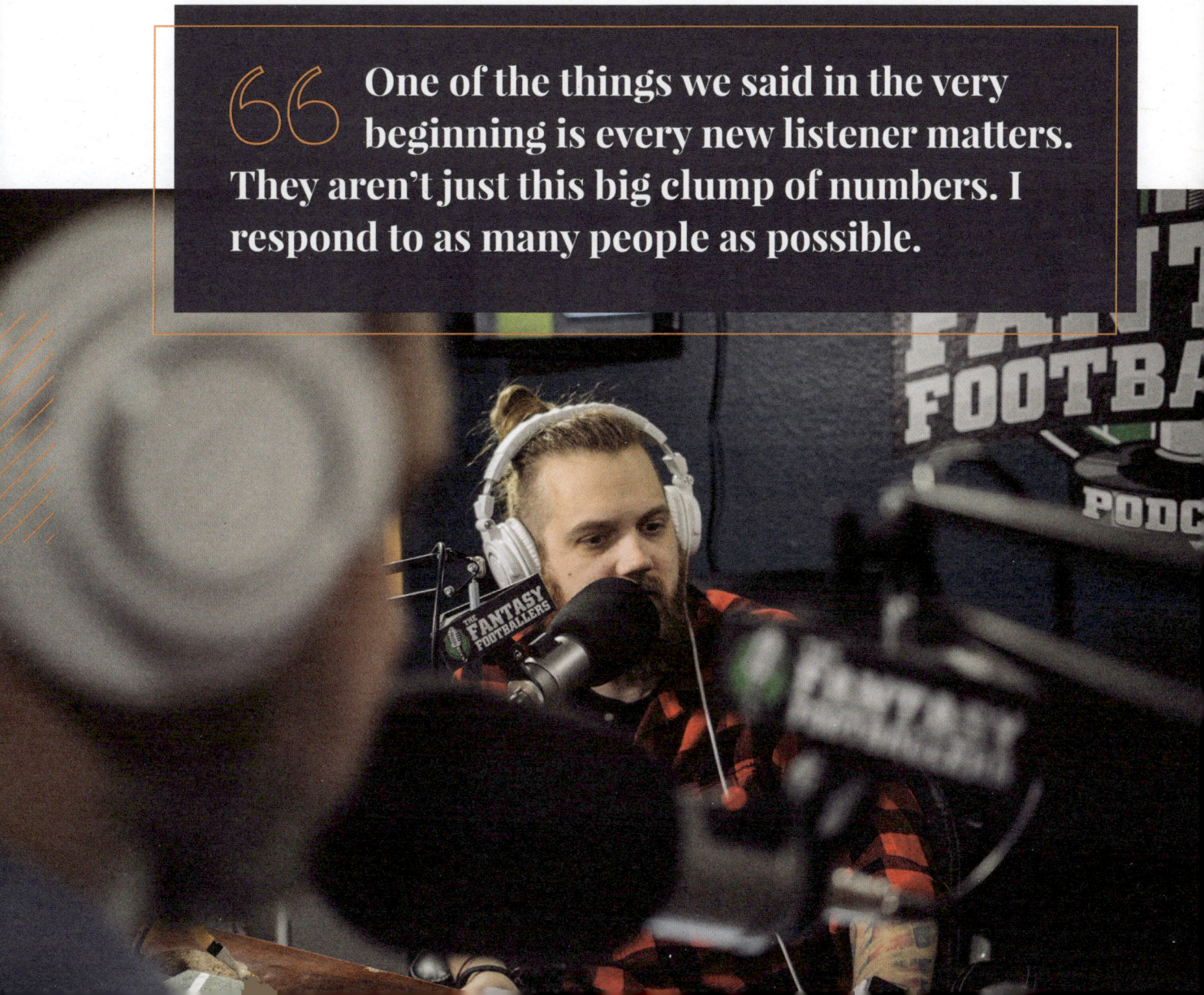

> *I think we all recognize that our wives do more work than we do.* —Andy

> *We thank our families big time for putting their trust in us. It has to be hard from their point of view—not only to have supported us, but also to keep doing it.* —Jason

Not only does their business provide stable income for all three families, but it also gives them the opportunity to share their favorite hobby with each other and with the world. Hearing stories and comments from their listeners fuels them to make the show better every season.

Looking at their current business model, they have three main sources of income that support the podcast in an even split. One-third is from advertising and sponsorships, while another third is from Patreon patrons. The last third is from digital products like the Ultimate Draft Kit.

The secret sauce to their success has really been how well they work together as a team. Because they're all proficient in separate areas, they've been able to define distinct roles within their business without stepping on each other's toes—most of the time.

Mike continues to do the show's audio editing and is the main person engaging with their community through social media and emails. Now that he's changed his mind-set from a freelancer to an equal business owner, he's proud to look back at the transformation he's made in just a few short years. After experimenting with a few different career paths, he's happy to have found what he wants to do with the rest of his life.

Jason works on the bigger advertising and sponsorship deals as the show owner. Being a part of *The Fantasy Footballers* has changed Jason's entire perspective on what it means to achieve success. He now puts family first in every pivotal business decision he makes and loves collaborating with Andy and Mike—and he never misses an opportunity to remind them that he's had the best overall accuracy in his drafts.

Andy, the "dad" of the group, continues to work on website development and other content creation projects while making sure the bills are paid. He's thankful to spend more time with his family now that he has stepped outside of the nine-to-five work environment. He wants to make his family proud and be present with his kids more than impressing others. Work-life balance will always be his top priority.

Now that their podcast attracts thousands of new listeners every month, Mike, Andy, and Jason have a lot to celebrate. Whenever they surpass a business goal, they splurge on a nice meal at Culver's. Because nothing says celebration like a ButterBurger combo meal shared with your best friends.

> **We thank our families big time for putting their trust in us. It has to be hard from their point of view—not only to have supported us, but also to keep doing it.**

The Business Today

Revenue Breakdown

40% Products   **30%** Advertising   **30%** Membership

By the Numbers

✉ **70,000**
Email subscribers

📇 **4,110**
Patreon supporters

Products & Services

- Ultimate Draft Kit
- Ultimate DFS Pass
- #FootClan membership
- Shirts and swag

Podcast Downloads per Year

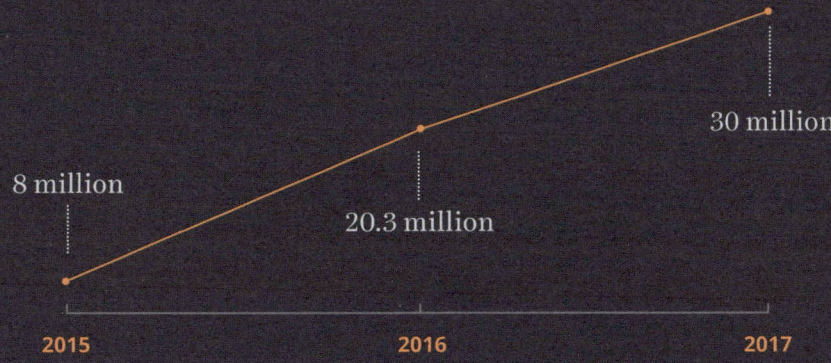

8 million (2015)   20.3 million (2016)   30 million (2017)

thefantasyfootballers.com

Patty Palmer

Mother. Wife. Art Teacher. Creative. Entrepreneur. Blogger.

WORDS BY KAYLA HOLLATZ • PHOTOGRAPHY BY DAVID SHERRY

As you step into Patty Palmer's Santa Barbara home, or even the family's cozy cottage in her hometown of Prince Edward Island, it's impossible to miss the bright-colored paintings and line drawings displayed in each room.

Patty has been drawing and creating art for as long as she can remember, but it's her own children's art that hangs proudly on her painted walls.

> *It brings me a lot of joy. There's something about children's art that is just so emotional, pure, and innocent. I'm incredibly attracted to that medium. The way children use paint and colors to express their little self . . . it makes me very happy.*

Most of Patty's own art has been tucked away in old sketchbooks, binders, and journals. Looking back at the colors and textures that fill each page, she's reminded of who she was as a child and who she still is today.

As an introverted, deeply creative child growing up on a farm, Patty saw art as an escape from the daily chores of farm life. When others picked up a basketball or softball, she picked up a colored pencil and chalk. She remembers drawing nearly every day as a child and into her teenage years.

Every piece of art she creates speaks to the vibrancy of her creative growth as an artist, teacher, and entrepreneur. Art has manifested itself in different ways throughout Patty's life, but her passion for entrepreneurship began with a fashion line.

Fashion Designer

After graduating from a three-year art school in Toronto, Patty moved back to Prince Edward Island and began working on the designs for her first business: manufacturing men's beach shorts.

> It taught me that no matter what my business idea was, it was worth trying. If the idea didn't work out, I could always recover using other skills I had.

In the 1980s, flashy swim trunks were in style, and Patty knew it was the perfect market to fit her artistic, quirky flair. Before selling her inventory at little island shops, she invested in an industrial sewing machine and set up shop in her bedroom.

After designing, sewing, and distributing hundreds of swim shorts, she knew it was time to expand her team. She sold her designs all over Canada before e-commerce was available, but then her business model started eating more cash than it could earn.

When she was twenty-five years old, she decided—after trying to increase her profit margins and lower her costs—to take a step back and close her business altogether. What others may have seen as failure, Patty saw as one of the best learning experiences she's ever had.

> *It taught me that no matter what my business idea was, it was worth trying. If the idea didn't work out, I could always recover using other skills I had.*

In her late twenties, she was inspired to start another clothing design business. Since quality golf wear selections for women were incredibly slim, she worked to close the gap in the market by manufacturing her unique designs.

Her golf wear business was born from a need to provide for herself after relocating from Prince Edward Island to California with her now husband. The business continued to thrive as she awaited her green card.

But when Patty and her husband decided it was time to start building their family a few years later, she closed the business and became a stay-at-home mom in Santa Barbara. She wasn't interested in pursuing fashion after having kids, but she began exercising her creativity in new ways that would eventually lead to her next step.

Stay-At-Home Mom and Art Teacher

For ten years, Patty was fiercely dedicated to instilling the value of artistic expression in her kids as a stay-at-home mom. She looks back on this time with gratitude and enjoyment, cherishing each arts and crafts project she was able to work on with her children.

During this time, she also volunteered on multiple educational committee boards and advocated for art programs. The elementary school that her kids attended didn't include art in the curriculum, so Patty volunteered her time and talents in the classroom.

1993 Closed her business and became a stay-at-home mom

After her youngest daughter went to kindergarten, Patty knew it was time to reenter the workforce. The very next week, a casual conversation with her close friend resulted in an introduction to a school principal.

Even though Patty hadn't worked full-time in ten years and didn't have a teaching degree, she and the principal thought she would be the perfect addition to the school as their new arts teacher. Working ten hours a week to start, Patty carved out another ten hours of lesson preparation time on top of her classroom hours.

Because the school had no arts curriculum, Patty was tasked with creating her own lesson plans from scratch. What may have made another educator's palms sweat made Patty even more excited to dive right in. While she admits to being overwhelmed at first, she quickly got the hang of creating lesson plans from scratch.

> *Creating the lessons was so fun. It was so rewarding for me to see how kids can be engaged by someone who's enthusiastic and who wants to teach them how to do art.*

The full creative freedom she had with creating the arts curriculum from the ground up gave birth to a blog—one that accidentally became a wildly successful business.

From Art Blogger to Profitable Online Business

Patty never started her blog as an innovative way to make money or even as a way to grow a large online following, although both happened within a few years.

Deep Space Sparkle, a blog name that was inspired by a Crayola crayon name, was initially created to share the artwork her students were creating in the classroom.

What she didn't expect was the large amount of fellow art teachers who began following along with her blog.

Inspired by what Patty was helping her students create, teachers asked her through blog comments for resources on how to teach the same subjects in their own classroom. Having a strong entrepreneurial background, Patty thought about how she could make side income with sales from these lesson plan PDFs.

> *I didn't have any pushback. Teachers were thrilled, and I'd sell lessons for $3 or $5. I would also include five lesson plans in a little PDF bundle.*

She never expected the low-priced PDF product sales to grow as fast as they did. In 2009, her first $5 PDF product, a fifteen-page Eric Carle seahorse lesson plan, generated $300 in its first month.

As Patty saw the income earning potential grow, she spent nearly all of her free time creating new lesson plans and testing them in the classroom. She quickly discovered which lessons were her students' favorites and which lessons didn't do as well.

By creating multiple PDF products each month, she grew her monthly shop sales to $2,000 in 2011. On top of her part-time teaching salary, Patty noticed just how quickly she had been able to create a viable income source for her family.

> *To add $2,000 a month to our family income was extraordinary . . . It gave us some freedom from our monthly expenses that come with three kids and a mortgage.*

> *It also made me a better teacher because I was meticulous about the words that I used, the strategies I employed, and the lessons I chose to give the students. And now I had a huge body of teachers looking to me to create an art curriculum for them and to help them in the classroom. It was a game changer.*

Seeing the income spike from her blog allowed Patty to think about not only what *Deep Space Sparkle* had grown into, but also what it could become. Having the childlike spirit of a dreamer, she went back to the drawing board and began approaching her blog like a true business.

From the very beginning, Patty wasn't interested in selling advertising space on her website, so she focused on creating her own products to sell. This served her community well and her blog traffic continued to grow with each month.

Transitioning Into Full-Time Entrepreneurship

After reaching a six-figure income from her blog in 2013, Patty began wondering if it was time to reassess where she spent her time. She loved being inside the classroom, but it started taking hours away from her business.

2013 Reached a six-figure income from *Deep Space Sparkle*

Instead of quitting both of her teaching jobs, she decided to let go of one position in order to teach two days a week instead of four. Her husband was a little nervous to have Patty quit the more stable job, but he believed in the vision she had for *Deep Space Sparkle*.

This decision gave Patty extra time to work on her blog, and her product sales doubled. She still couldn't believe how quickly her blog was growing, but she wasn't ready to give up on teaching yet.

> *The classroom was my experiment. It was the home base for my business, and I thought I needed that to create my business and the products. I thought if I wasn't teaching, I wouldn't have a product.*

Patty held onto this idea tightly until she received the opportunity of a lifetime. As a child, Patty had always dreamed of writing a children's book. Earlier in life, she spent over a decade reaching out to agents and editors—and now she had them coming to her.

While the opportunity to write a book seemed like a dream come true, she knew it would require a sacrifice. The idea of writing a book while running her business and teaching children at school created an overwhelming sense of chaos.

She saw this as a sign to retire from teaching in 2015 so she could focus on writing a book and running *Deep Space Sparkle* full-time. Because Patty loved her students and teaching, it wasn't an easy transition, but her other creative projects were just as important to her.

> " The classroom was my experiment. It was the home base for my business, and I thought I needed that to create my business and the products. I thought if I wasn't teaching, I wouldn't have a product.

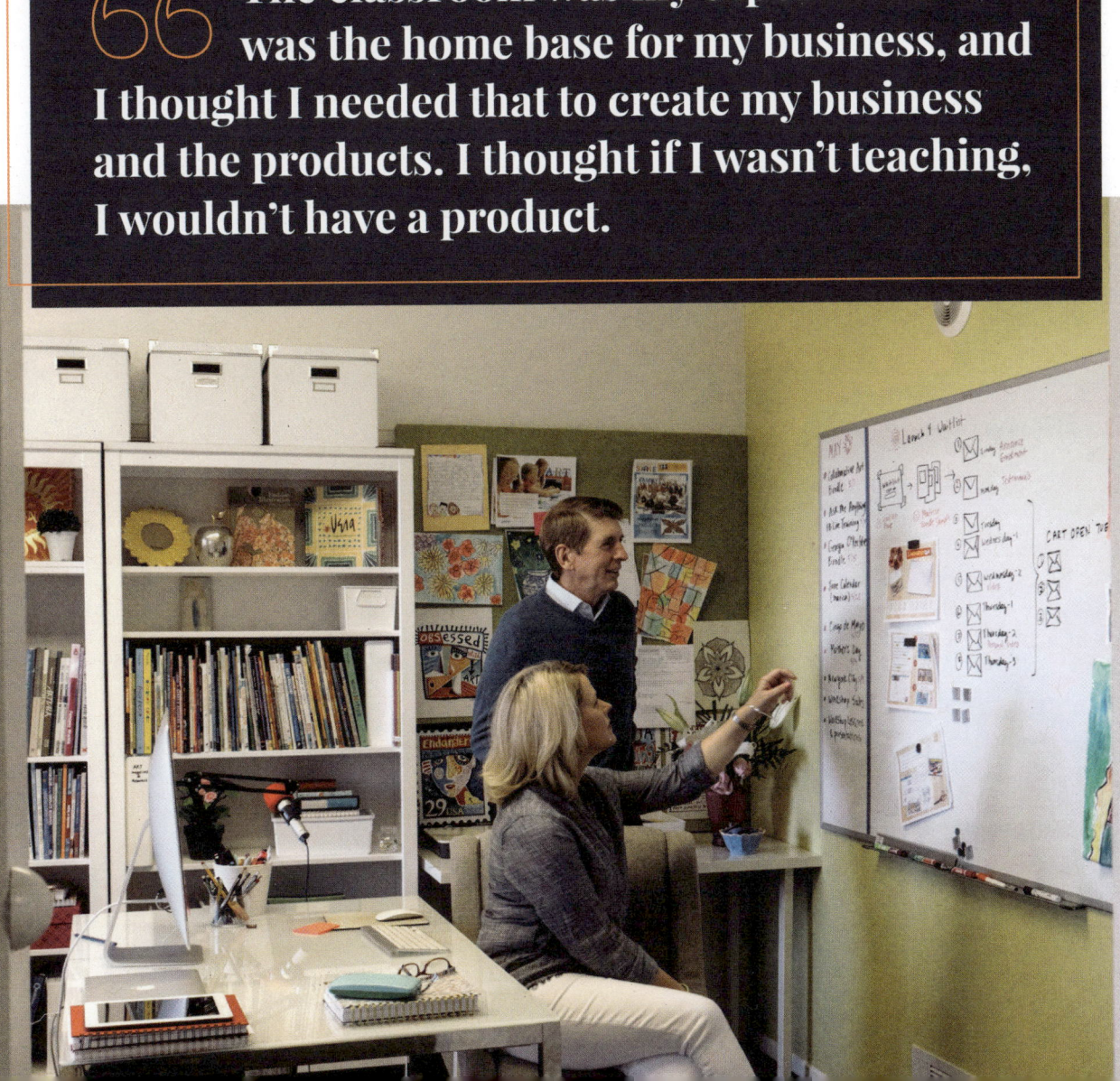

> Making the mental shift from wearing all the hats in her business to choosing which hats were the best fit was the hardest change Patty had to make.

Patty's Business Model Today

When Patty's lesson plan library reached 300 products, she decided to radically change her business model. Instead of offering her PDFs for $5 each, she would bundle them all together and offer them inside a membership community.

A membership community would give art teachers the chance to access all of Patty's lesson plans for a low recurring monthly fee.

Knowing this business model shift would create a great amount of work, Patty's husband decided to quit his computer engineering job to work full-time on *Deep Space Sparkle*. In addition to Patty and her husband working on the blog and membership community, they also hired four employees in 2017.

Now the membership community generates about 80% of the blog's income. The other 20% comes from single-purchased PDFs and workshops.

Making the mental shift from wearing all the hats in her business to choosing which hats were the best fit was the hardest change Patty had to make. Many entrepreneurs find it difficult to loosen the reins and hand control of business projects to other team members, but Patty recommends practicing this skill early.

> *It's been about eight months in the process of shifting from working in my business organically . . . to doing things when it fits into my life, to developing the systems to run the business. This means making sure the team can handle parts of the business so that I can step into the visionary role.*

Patty recently handed off the project of writing a weekly newsletter to her assistant, something she never imagined outsourcing. It ended up creating a great sense of relief because it allowed Patty to refocus on creating valuable content and in-person experiences at her studio in Santa Barbara.

Her business now gives her more room to make time for what truly matters. Since her kids are now grown up and in college, Patty defines the "good life" as coming home on a casual Friday night to make pizza in the kitchen with her husband. He's in charge of picking up the wine while she makes homemade dough. It's the perfect way to end a successful week of business together.

When Patty reflects on the success of her business, she smiles and attributes its growth to her lack of expectations for what it would become.

> *I didn't have to write a business plan and state my intentions to the world. I grew* Deep Space Sparkle *organically and authentically. I was really coming from a place of helping teachers teach art to kids in a better way or in a way that's best for them. I wanted to make them happier in the classroom, so kids can walk into a classroom and feel good about themselves. That has always been my goal, and it continues to be my mission.*

From an early age, Patty recognized an innate desire in herself to create something, a sense of yearning we all share. She made it her mission to inspire art teachers, students, and parents to exercise their own creativity on a daily basis through art exploration.

She inspires us to make room for play and never lose our childlike sense of wonder.

Now it's your turn to pick up a paintbrush and create something new.

The Business Today

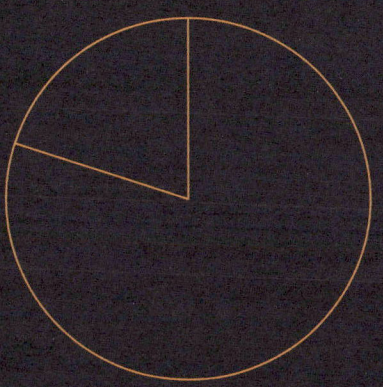

Revenue Breakdown

80%
Membership community

20%
Digital product downloads

By the Numbers

250,000
Monthly blog readers

85,000
Email subscribers

6
People working on *Deep Space Sparkle*

4,000
Members in Sparklers Members Club

Products & Services

- Sparklers Members Club art teacher membership community
- Art bundles and lesson plans
- Online workshops

2009
Income from first month of sales
$300

2011
Monthly shop income
$2,000

deepspacesparkle.com

Joshua Becker

Christian. Husband. Father. Writer. Minimalist. Blogger.

WORDS BY KAYLA HOLLATZ • PHOTOGRAPHY BY BRANDON SULLIVAN

Rummaging through the stacks of piled cardboard boxes in his driveway, Joshua Becker settled into an afternoon of organizing the mess in front of him. Among the skyscrapers of boxes were loose tools and garden supplies that needed to be taken to the backyard where his five-year-old son was swinging cheerfully on their playground.

Just then, Joshua caught a glimpse from the corner of his eye: a neighbor was walking toward him. He stepped away from the boxes, wiped the sweat from his forehead, and smiled at her.

After exchanging pleasantries, Joshua shifted the conversation toward the towering cardboard boxes that were impossible to miss.

Looking at him sympathetically, she said two lines that would forever change his life.

> *You know, that's why my daughter is a minimalist. She keeps telling me I don't need to own all this stuff.*

Joshua immediately thought of his son playing alone in the backyard. He questioned why he wasn't playing with his son instead of spending the weekend organizing things he didn't truly need.

> *Everything I owned was actually taking me away from the very thing that brings me happiness, purpose, and fulfillment in life, which I think is the key realization of minimalism.*

Inspired by his neighbor, he decided to take a deeper look into minimalism. As he talked to his wife about what a minimalist lifestyle would mean for their family, they decided to pursue this new stage of life together. It was a brand-new beginning for the Becker family, but it would take months of decluttering and minimizing to reverse their mind-set.

This season of refinement inspired a blog, which became a personal journal of the family's minimalism progress. It now attracts over one million readers every month, but Joshua's journey to full-time blogging and minimalism started well before he published his first blog post.

Transitioning Career Paths

Coming from a conservative, spiritual upbringing in a small Midwestern town, Joshua was instilled with the values of faith, family, and friendship from a very young age.

Joshua doesn't remember ever having dreams of running a business or making a living through writing. Instead, he focused much of his attention on sports, desperately wanting to keep up with his athletic brother.

> **Everything I owned was actually taking me away from the very thing that brings me happiness, purpose, and fulfillment.**

Playing sports at a small high school in Wahpeton, North Dakota, meant he was able to play on any team he desired. Joshua's competitive nature was cultivated on the tennis and basketball court. Along with being dedicated to sports and his schoolwork, he also grew up in the church.

As he approached high school graduation, Joshua became increasingly interested in pursuing a college degree in banking and finance, allowing him to follow in his father's footsteps. He recalls the goal of being a stock analyst on Wall Street or a banker who gives multimillion dollar loans to corporations rising to the top of his aspirations list.

However, throughout college, Joshua's faith shifted from an accepted family tradition to a more personal relationship with God. He was mentored by a youth pastor who inspired him to live a life of faith beyond Sunday services. The more Joshua uncovered his faith, the less attached he felt to the dream of working in banking and finance.

> *When I had a year left of college, I decided to be a pastor instead. I thought, "I can do the banking thing, but man, I want to be for other kids what that pastor was to me. I just want to speak into kids' lives, help them see the potential they have, and help them discover what life can mean.*

In the following year, Joshua finished his undergraduate degree in banking and finance at the University of Nebraska Omaha, and then pursued a two-year internship in youth ministry in the fall.

Youth Pastor and Blogger

After the two-year internship, newly married Joshua relocated with his wife to Wisconsin to become a youth pastor. While he was pastoring there, he also enrolled in a master's program in theological studies from Bethel Seminary in St. Paul, Minnesota.

> *In my theological degree, there were more personal transformation and leadership conversations that took place, as opposed to the finance degree.*

What started as a way for Joshua to learn and process through this significant life change turned into an accidental platform to serve other people who were struggling with consumerism.

Joshua spent the next five years as a youth pastor in Wisconsin before moving to Vermont. It was there that he accepted another youth pastor position that would last six years.

The minimalist-inspired conversation he had with his neighbor happened during his time in Vermont. Still working as a pastor, Joshua started his blog, *Becoming Minimalist*, to document his family's journey to living a minimalist life.

For Joshua, the blog was like a public journal where he kept record of his family's decluttering experiments and his own reflections on minimalism. What started as a way for Joshua to learn and process through this significant life change turned into an accidental platform to serve other people who were struggling with consumerism.

He never dreamed of pursuing the blog full-time when he started it, but when the idea first surfaced two years later, he would spend over three years deciding if it was the right move for him and his family.

> I'm a pastor because I think God wants me to be pastoring. I'm not doing that unless I think God's calling me to do it. I asked myself, "Does God want me to stop pastoring to run a blog? Who stops pastoring to be a blogger? What am I? Crazy?"

Transitioning Into Full-Time Blogging

For a year and a half, Joshua spent time seeking the advice of mentors he trusted, knowing he had the unshakeable support of his wife throughout the entire process.

Even though he was feeling called out of youth ministry, he didn't know if the next step was full-time blogging. Nothing felt right about the traditional job search process, including writing a new resume, so he picked up the phone and called a close friend.

While explaining his dilemma, his friend suggested taking a temporary two-year position at another church to give himself space to explore full-time blogging. Immediately, Joshua felt a rush of calm and knew it felt like a good option.

Two years would give him enough time to discover if God was really calling him to pursue *Becoming Minimalist* full-time, so he accepted a new associate pastor position in Phoenix, Arizona.

This also gave his family the chance to downsize their $315,000 house in Vermont to a $165,000 house in Arizona providing them more room to maneuver financially. The family's minimalism journey was still going strong, and everyone in the family was ready for a fresh start in Phoenix.

While in Phoenix, Joshua noticed that he was becoming more and more passionate about the message of the blog. Readers were commenting about how much his journey had inspired their own and were asking for even more resources.

As Joshua felt more of his creative energy naturally flowing to the blog, he also saw how much work was involved in maintaining the audience he had amassed over the five years of blogging. He couldn't keep up with emails, messages, blog writing, and social media in addition to his full-time ministry position.

As more income was generated from the blog, he decided to step away from his ministry job to pursue *Becoming Minimalist* full-time in 2013.

How Minimalism and Generosity Intersect

In the beginning, Joshua felt minimalism was heavily tied to decluttering. That was the most tangible form of minimalism he had discovered at the time. He started by getting rid of things he didn't need, donating them to Goodwill by loading the boxes that were once in his driveway into his van.

He quickly saw that this decluttering process raised an even bigger question: *How did I accumulate all of this stuff?*

> *Why are Americans so stressed out about money? Seventy-two percent of Americans have financial-related stress, and yet we all have enough money. We're one of the wealthiest nations in the history of the world. Why are all of us worried about money? We have a roof, we have food, we have clothes, and we have televisions. We have more stuff than we need. Why are worried about money?*

He found that in our consumerist culture, we heavily rely on advertisements and other people to tell us what will make us happy. By searching for happiness in material possessions, we miss out on cherishing the things that will actually bring us fulfillment.

Using this inspiration, Joshua wrote a book proposal for what would become his first traditionally published book, *The More of Less*. Many publishers loved the message of the book and were attracted to the large blog audience Joshua had already built. These two factors led to multiple offers from publishers.

As the book offers began to climb, Joshua was faced with a life-changing decision. Would he accept the highest offer and pocket the cash from the book advance or would he funnel the money into a bigger cause?

Generosity had always been one of Joshua's highest values, especially as a Christian, but he felt tension when looking at the high-paying book offers.

> *When the final numbers for the book came in, I said to my wife, "Do I really believe everything I said? Do I really believe that I'm going to find more happiness and more security in being generous with my money than keeping it for myself?"*
>
> *It's one thing to write that when you don't have any money, and it's another thing to write it when you have the money and the temptation is there to keep it all to yourself. That's when we said, "No, we believe it. It's true."*

When looking for causes to donate to, he revisited a passion for adoption that he and his wife had always shared. His wife was adopted, and Joshua also had a heart for orphan care, but they never felt a calling to adopt themselves.

Since Joshua was interested in becoming a bigger ally for adoption, he talked with a friend who had recently adopted two

2016 First traditionally published book

children. Joshua asked him what he could do to help, and his friend said the largest need is in funding orphanages around the world.

Joshua's friend noted how difficult it is for orphans to grow up in poorly run, poorly funded orphanages where neglect and abuse can go undocumented. Joshua could be a beacon of light and help by building orphanages that function more like a family than dormitory housing institutions.

This lit a fire in Joshua that burned brighter than any calling he had ever experienced. Knowing that orphan care would resonate with his blog audience, no matter what their faith background was, he decided to use 75% of the book advance to start a nonprofit under the name The Hope Effect.

> *Generosity had become such an important theme on* Becoming Minimalist *as I noticed how generosity was impacting and influencing my life. I found greater fulfillment and happiness in giving things away than holding onto them.*

With one orphanage already funded in Honduras, The Hope Effect team is continuing to raise money for several other orphanages with the same family-style home model. With 100% of the nonprofit organization's donations going straight into the housing and care programs, Joshua is changing how the world cares for orphans.

Joshua's Business Model

When Joshua reflects on his journey to full-time blogging, he is filled with gratitude for the platform he's cultivated for over seven years. His generosity is contagious, and he's inspiring a whole new generation of bloggers who want to make a living through blogging while making a difference.

His passion for the mission of *Becoming Minimalist* and The Hope Effect continues to grow as his audience reaches new heights. With one million readers visiting his blog every month, he spends more energy than ever creating valuable content both for people inside the minimalist movement and those outside.

As his readership increases, his monthly income has also increased. He currently makes around $2000 every month from his self-published books and another $3000 each month from affiliate sales. Speaking gigs earn him anywhere from $1000 to $4000 a month.

The book contract for *The More of Less* has by far generated the most amount of income, bringing in $300,000—most of which was used to fund his nonprofit organization.

His online course, titled Uncluttered, brought in $200,000 in its first year. It is expected to be the website's biggest revenue driver for years to come.

> **With 100% of the nonprofit organization's donations going straight into the housing and care programs, Joshua is changing how the world cares for orphans.**

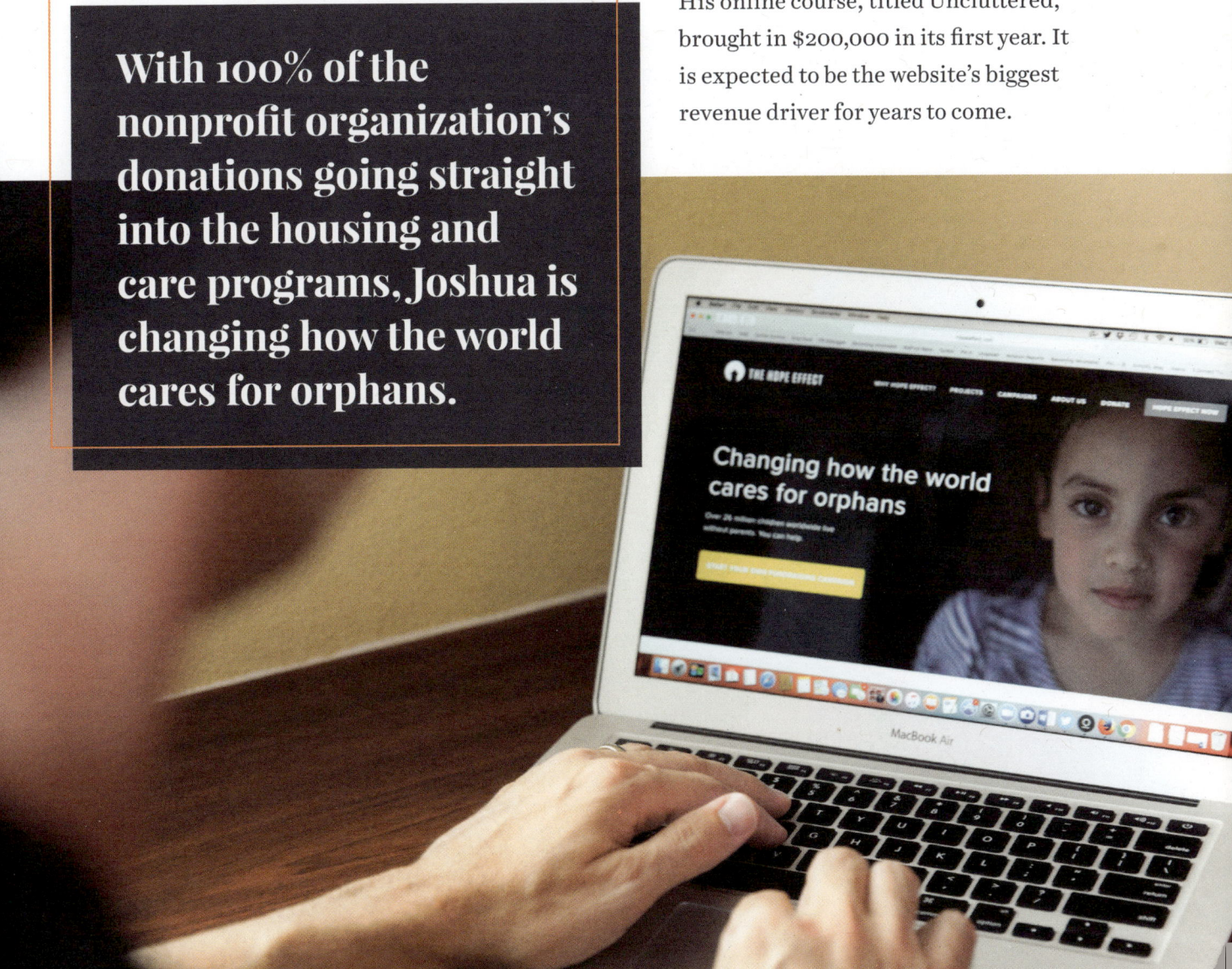

Joshua is a bright light for those who want to make a living doing something that matters while funding causes they believe in. When asked what blogging means to him, he said it has changed his perspective of and the way he interacts with the world around him.

| *I think blogging made me far more observant to life around me.*

After downsizing his home, donating most of his possessions to Goodwill, starting a nonprofit, and pursuing his blog full-time, Joshua is happier than ever before.

On any given weekend afternoon, you can now find him relaxing with his family in the backyard—with no cardboard boxes in sight.

The Business Today

Revenue Breakdown

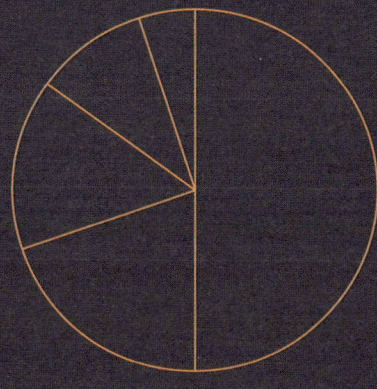

50% Courses
20% Books
15% Magazines
10% Public speaking
5% Affiliate sales

FEBRUARY 2010
First month generating income
$700

OCTOBER 2013
First month full time
$5,200

By the Numbers

$200,000
Income generated by online course *Uncluttered* in its first year

1,000,000
Unique website visitors per month

155,000
Email subscribers

Products & Services

- Uncluttered course
- *Simplify* Magazine
- *The More of Less* book
- *Simplify* book
- *Clutterfree with Kids* book
- Public speaking
- *The Minimalist Home* book (December 2018)

becomingminimalist.com

CONCLUSION

When I started my blog, I didn't know that I could earn a living from it. Technically, I knew it was possible to earn a living from a blog—and I could point out examples of people who did, but they were more famous, talented, or successful. It was possible for those people, but that didn't mean it was possible for me.

Obviously, if you already have 100,000 readers on your site, you can sell a book or course. But what if you are just getting your first 100 readers?

On March 20, 2012, two bloggers changed my entire perspective.

A designer in Colorado named Jarrod Drysdale launched a book called *Bootstrapping Design*. At the same time—on the other side of the world in Japan—Sacha Greif launched a book on user interface design. They didn't coordinate—they didn't even know each other. It was just by chance.

In the first forty-eight hours they made $8,753 and $6,663, respectively.

Those numbers opened an entirely new world to me. Not because they were so large, but because I could relate to Sacha and Jarrod.

They didn't make hundreds of thousands of dollars launching a product to massive audiences. Instead, they launched great products to small audiences—an audience that felt achievable. Most importantly, they were designers just like me.

If they could do it, I could too.

My hope is that in reading *I Am a Blogger*, you had a similar experience where you found a story you could connect with, someone who was close enough to your industry, opportunity, or values that inspired you. Maybe they showed you that you could build an audience and earn a living.

Thanks to Sacha and Jarrod, I went on to provide for my family entirely through my writing and blogging—and, ultimately, ended up building Seva into a platform that helps over 20,000 creators to do the same.

I hope that *I Am a Blogger* would be a similar spark for you. A year from now, you could be following in the footsteps of these remarkable people who are earning a great living for their families and making an impact on their readers.

But before you close this book and start on this new journey, I need to let you know something really important: this will be harder and take longer than you think.

So many people begin an idea entirely based on their motivation, and then they lose momentum when the interest is gone. With the wrong expectations, you'll scrap these dreams within a few months. I don't want that to happen.

Instead, know that this is going to take consistent effort over time. As my friend Sean McCabe says,

> *Show up every day for two years.*

It will be hard. It will take time. And it will be worth it.

Go.

Create something magical.

Earn a living from it.

And at the next family reunion when your grandma asks what you are doing now proudly say,

> *I am a blogger.*

■ *Nathan Barry*
   CEO of Seva

ACKNOWLEDGMENTS

This book, along with the short documentaries that accompany its original publication, are the truest form of a labor of love.

As a software company, it can be so easy to stay focused solely on income and tactics to help grow the business—just like the shallow stories that miss so much of what leads to a blogger's success. We've managed to continue to grow as a company while also maintaining the heart and soul of what makes us who we are: our mission to help creators earn a living.

First of all, we have to thank the creators who opened their homes and shared their lives with us in order to make this project possible: Andy, Asad, Barron, Brooke, Chad, Corey, Courtney, Crosby, Dave, Jason, Joshua, Krista, Mike, Mique, Patty, Sarah, Tyler, and Vanessa—thank you. Your stories inspire us every day, and the way you approach your work with purpose and care sets an example for the rest of us.

The creators included in this book are just a small sample of the thousands of creators—nearly 20,000 at the time of this writing—who trust us with their business and give us the privilege of serving them every day. Without our customers at Seva, we would be nothing. This book would not exist, our almost forty teammates would not have jobs, and we would not get to pursue this mission of helping creators earn a living. Thank you for being our fuel and inspiration.

Without the courage and vision of our founder, Nathan Barry, projects like *I Am a Blogger* would never see the light of day. If we hadn't first invested nearly $50,000 of the company's money in traveling the country, filming interviews, hiring talented photographers, and producing this book and films, well, there would be no book or films. When there is no logical business case for projects like this, Nathan gives us permission to do it anyway because it's a reflection of who we are and who we want to be.

The Seva team is made up of servant leaders and badass professionals who care deeply about this work. While the teammates who made this book had direct input on the words, the design, and everything else, the rest of the team was building software, answering support tickets, and doing the hard work required to support creators in pursuing work that matters: Adam J., Adam M., Alexis, Ashley, Brad, Brendan, Bruno, Christina, Cory, Derrick, Dylan, Elizabeth, Erin, Grant, Haley C., Haley J., Isa, Johnny, Jon, Jure, Marc, Matt, Miguel, Morgan, Newbill, Nicole, Noel, Pier-Olivier, Renee, Ruslan, Semonna, Steven, and Tyler—this project is just one piece of this special thing we're building together. Let's hope that as we continue to grow, we feel even a fraction of the joy we'll feel someday in the future when we look back at all we've accomplished on this journey together.

To the small but mighty full-time team that has brought this project to life—wow. Wow, wow, wow. What you are capable of doing with so few resources and so little time is absolutely amazing. You have made a beautiful work of art, and I hope you will display it proudly wherever you live. This is a reflection of what you are capable of. Thank you, Charli and Dani. You are remarkable human beings.

We also had a wonderful group of contractors who played every bit as big of a role as our team in making this project come to life. Caleb Wojcik and Tim Krupa from Caleb Wojcik Films traveled the country with us to film the documentaries and took photographs for nine of the sixteen stories in this book. Kayla Hollatz is the author of fifteen of the sixteen stories in this book, and she completed them on tight deadline with the utmost professionalism and a smile on her face. Our editor on this project was Amanda Johnson. She brought a consistent style and voice to the entire project, while helping us stick to our word counts without losing meaning or storyline. We also worked with a number of photographers to capture the beautiful imagery throughout this book: Brandon Sullivan, David Sherry, Joshua Fortuna, Kambria Fischer, Mark Forbes, Maureen Cotton and Yesenia Fortuna.

■ *Barrett Brooks*
  COO of Seva

We launched this project on Kickstarter to help us get it across the finish line. To all of the backers of our first-ever Kickstarter project: thank you! We want to especially call out and thank those backers that donated $500 or more:

Andrew Morgan

BJ Wright

Jevonnah Ellison

Lisa Cressman

Matthew Gartland

Nicole Walters

Pat Flynn

Paul Zanetti

Peter Hulce

Tony Rulli

& Adobe Creative Cloud

Thank you for making this project possible with such generous support.

For more about the *I Am a Blogger* project and to watch the videos, visit **iamablogger.co**